WRITING ACROSS THE CURRICULUM
BECAUSE ALL TEACHERS TEACH WRITING

Shelley S. Peterson

PORTAGE & MAIN PRESS

Portage and Main Press acknowledges the financial support of the Government of Canada through the Book Publishing Industry Development Program (BPIDP) for our publishing activities.

Printed and bound in Canada by Friesens

05 06 07 08 09 5 4 3 2 1

Library and Archives Canada Cataloguing in Publication

Peterson, Shelley

   Writing across the curriculum : because all teachers teach writing / Shelley Peterson.

Includes bibliographical references.

ISBN 1-55379-060-X

   1. English language--Composition and exercises--Study and teaching (Elementary). 2. Language arts--Correlation with content subjects.

I. Title.

LB1576.P48 2005   372.62'3044   C2005-906881-7

 PORTAGE &
MAIN PRESS

100 – 318 McDermot Ave.
Winnipeg, MB
Canada R3A 0A2

Tel: 204-987-3500
Toll-free: 1-800-667-9673
Toll-free fax: 1-866-734-8477
Email: books@portageandmainpress.com

CONTENTS

CHAPTER 1

WRITING AND LEARNING ACROSS THE CURRICULUM

I write because I don't know what
I think until I read what I say.
(Flannery O'Conner in Murray 1990, p.8)

THE VALUE OF WRITING ACROSS THE CURRICULUM

Many of you teach it all. You paddle alongside your students down a river of reading/writing/viewing/listening/speaking, across the lake of "Greece, an Ancient Civilization," through the stream of "Force and Motion" and countless other topics within the grade-level curriculum. Across all the subject areas, you may find that there is so much for students to learn and so little time in the school day to do the learning. The problem is not having lots to learn – it can be rather exciting, really. Finding a way to accomplish everything within the confines of a classroom schedule is a constant challenge, however.

Some of you specialize in and teach one subject area to a large number of students. You already see the value of writing in your subject – for example, it helps students learn concepts and skills in context, and it helps students develop organizational skills. Yet, with the limited time you have to teach the concepts, writing can seem like an add-on – one more thing to add to the long list of things you need to achieve in the day. Finding time for students to write is a challenge. Finding time to assess and grade all the writing is another challenge altogether. You envision the stacks of papers from the hundreds of students you teach each week, and the idea of having students write more can be daunting.

This book is intended for those teachers who teach in the language arts or in English, and also for those teachers who are content-area specialists in history, geography, math, science, health, French, and so on. You will find ideas for teaching and assessing writing in content areas; ideas that take into account the challenges of your teaching context and the limits to your time.

WHY IS THIS BOOK IMPORTANT?

In a world where information multiplies at dazzling rates and is available from a multitude of sources, being able to make sense of information is a basic skill. In daily life, we are not only expected to know; we are also expected to communicate what we know. Learning and being able to write about what is learned are increasingly important in contemporary life and in what we imagine life will be for our students when they become adults. Policymakers recognize this. The significance of writing and content learning is clearly stated in new provincial and state guidelines for school curricula at all levels.

Content-area subjects provide students with real-life questions and ideas that they can explore in their writing. Content-area subjects can be a goldmine for possibilities to help teach students about the functions of writing. Students develop questioning and problem-solving skills and attitudes in the content-area subjects that help them to become better writers. Writing in the content-area subjects teaches students about effective communication with a variety of audiences, and about organizing ideas. The idea of writing across the curriculum is to show students that they do not have to be in language arts classes to play with the words, rhymes, and rhythms of poetry, or to develop dialogue for a play. They can do all of these things while writing about science concepts, or historical facts. In other words, as students are learning about the content-area concepts within each subject, they can also be developing as writers.

Content areas introduce students to genres in writing as they are used in real-life contexts. When students read explanations for creating a pulley system in their science class, for example, they see how explanations are written and can use these explanations as models for their own writing. Similarly, students who are involved in a social studies unit on municipal government have a depth of information and a wealth of resources to write a letter to the editor of a local newspaper.

Students generally show great enthusiasm for writing brochures, narratives, and poems. Completing short-answer and note-taking assignments generate far less interest.

The motivation for writing is not just in completing tasks that the students find enjoyable, but also in the value that writing holds outside the classroom. Researchers (Brandt and Graff 2005), who look at workplace literacy skills tell us that writing is becoming, more than ever before, a critically important literacy skill. Success in workplaces of the future will be contingent upon being able to communicate information from a number of sources such as web sites, books, articles, interviews, and CDs, which are usually written. Integrating writing instruction into content areas helps students develop effective writing skills and an attitude that writing is an important part of many activities in their daily lives.

Discovery Writing

This book is based on the view that writing is a process that helps learners think more deeply about ideas and information they encounter when reading, listening, viewing, and moving throughout their worlds. This thinking leads to a fuller and better understanding of the information and ideas.

When I say that writing helps students to think, I am referring to the writing of stories, essays, poems, or any whole piece of writing for which students have some control over the format, topic, purpose, and audience – what I call *discovery writing*. Discovery writing helps students make sense of the rolling, backtracking highway of thoughts running through their heads. The written words, phrases, sentences, and paragraphs give thoughts some shape and form. As Flannery O'Conner expresses in the quote at the beginning of this chapter, the very act of searching for words and then rubbing them up against each other create spaces for new understandings to emerge.

Emig (1983) explains that in order to write, students' thoughts have to slow down to allow their hands to capture them as they write or type. Slowing down their thinking "allows for surprise, time for the unexpected to intrude and even take over" (p.112). The discovery and deep thinking rarely happen when students are asked to fill in blanks, copy notes from a blackboard, or provide short answers to questions. Although these types of writing can be helpful for gathering information to compose a more sustained piece of writing, they generally do not lend themselves to wild sparks of creativity or deep pools of focused thought.

Wood Ray (2001) writes that short answers or learning log entries are "a piece of cake compared to developing an argument convincingly for an audience" (p.21). They are not as demanding as discovery writing. In my own elementary classrooms, I found that students needed more support to carry out the discovery writing because of the greater demands. In the following chapters, different strategies for providing such support will be explained, and helpful mini-lessons will show teachers how to help their students become comfortable writing in several genres.

As we all know, discovery writing takes time. Exciting new ideas and deeper understandings are not likely to leap out at students when they plan, write, revise, and edit their writing in just two 40-minute science periods. Writing instruction may begin as a content-area unit begins and continue throughout the unit, taking up 15-20 minutes of many content classes throughout the unit. Writing instruction may also happen in blocks, as teachers devote a number of content classes to writing. Teachers may choose to use the time set aside in language arts classes and their writers workshops to work on the content-area writing. In chapter 2, the issue of finding time to dedicate to writing is addressed.

When we integrate writing into content areas there are two main goals. First, integration helps to reinforce the concepts, and, second it helps improve students' writing abilities. We have to trust that students will benefit from the time devoted to the many processes and concerns of writing. We have to believe that writing deepens our students' learning, and that there is the magnificent possibility that writing will expand our students' sense of who they are and all that life has to offer. Students can use the writing they do in any subject area to explore their worlds and come to know more about themselves in the process. Within any subject area, the time devoted to writing has greater benefits than can be captured in any list of curriculum objectives.

Leonora, a grade-eight science teacher, says that her students' narrative writing about pulleys helped them to "think about what potential things can happen outside the class lesson." One of her students agreed, saying, "It feels like it pays off more when you finish because it seems like you did more."On top of learning more, another student found the experience enjoyable: "It was kind of easier to learn because she put it in a way that was fun for us."

ISSUES IN CONTENT-AREA WRITING

A number of issues arise when students write longer answers and learning log responses in content classes.

- How much freedom should students have to choose the format, genre, topic, and tone for their content-area writing?

- How much emphasis should be placed on writing conventions in content-area writing?

- What should teachers assess in content-area writing?

Each question could generate hours of interesting conversations among educators. The following provides a basis for those conversations to happen. Greater depth on these topics is provided in later chapters.

To many of us, when we start to think about writing in content areas we recall images of writing a report on a particular country in social studies class, or writing about an animal in science classes. Content-area writing can be so much more than that. Instead, consider the possibility that students might write on any topic they choose using whatever genre and tone that they think is appropriate for their topic. Students use their imaginations, knowledge bases, and interests to help them incorporate what they have learned in the unit. The only constraint we place on their writing is that it has to be about a particular unit of study in a content area. With such loosely-drawn parameters, there is great scope for students to write in any genre they want: narrative, non-narrative, poetry, cartoon, and so on. They are free to write in a way that they find personally meaningful and enjoyable.

Some may argue that students' ownership of their writing could be lost in content writing because students are more intent on demonstrating their content knowledge. Introducing a content-area writing task into a writers workshop, for example, may mean that students have less choice for their writing time. Yet, my experience with grade six and eight science students shows that students appreciate having loose parameters set on their writing. In a way it helps the students narrow down and focus their writing more easily. My students thought first about what they wanted to write. In the back of their minds, students remembered that they had to show what they knew about the science concepts. Foremost in their minds, just as in a writers workshop, the students' main concerns were making sure they could fit in all they wanted to say and their audience's response. In these classes, students no longer struggled to find a topic for their writing as students so often do in open-choice writers workshops. With a well-defined topic already in place, students have a starting point from which to imagine and create.

In addition, researchers such as Timothy Lensmire (1994), Margaret Finders (1997), and Brett Elizabeth Blake (1997), and myself (Peterson 2003) question how "free" the free-choice writing in open-choice writers workshop really is. We have found that the assumptions and values of the classroom social network sometimes constrain students' topic choices. Students try to stay within the parameters of what peers consider acceptable, and they often write using stereotypical views of gender and social class. I have found that peers ridicule the one student who voluntarily decides to go against peer expectations in choosing his/her topic for writing. For the most part, I observed that students aligned their writing with what their peers' expected in order to avoid social embarrassment. Given the narrower choice of topics in content-area writing, this kind of social determination no longer plays a role in students' writing.

Teachers who create loose boundaries for students' writing choices in content areas implicitly give students permission to try something that might interest the individual student, even if it goes against prevailing assumptions within the peer social network. Peers do not ridicule students who try something new in writing about content-area topics in the same way because the student is writing within expectations set by the teacher, not choosing a topic entirely on his/her own.

Another issue to consider in content-area writing is the degree of attention that teachers should pay to students' use of spelling, punctuation, and grammar – the basic writing conventions. Many of our students spend countless hours blogging, e-mailing, and text messaging. Compared to generations past, the students now have more opportunities in their daily lives to write. To communicate effectively, students have a very strong social motivation to write. The joys they experience through this socially oriented writing carry into other parts of their writing lives. The problem with these types of written communication is that the writing itself is not conventional. Informal, shortened, phonetic spellings of words, symbols with meanings that most teachers might not understand, and sentence structures that follow "techno-standards," not writing conventions, are the norm for these communication methods. Students write more than they used to, but the kind of writing is drastically changed. They may need their teacher's guidance to recognize that the informal tone, spelling, grammar, and punctuation that they use when writing e-mails are not appropriate in their formal writing in other contexts. We need to help students recognize that different contexts and different audiences may require writing to take on a different form and voice. In a more formal setting, writing will not be appropriate if it does not follow the conventions. This means that reinforcing the appropriate use of writing conventions is as necessary in our science classes as it is in our language classes. In this way, students get the message that effective communication is important in every part of their world – both with their friends and family, and in school.

It is often the case that students are easily able to *talk* about their understanding of concepts in science, social studies, or health, but have difficulty *writing* what they know. How can teachers help their students communicate their knowledge both in writing and orally, with equal ease and ability? This dilemma leads to the question of assessing the content-area writing that students submit to teachers. Some may argue against assessing the basic writing skills when marking content writing, for fear that it will overshadow the need for students to understand the concepts. They suggest that students' grades reflect their understanding of the concepts, not their literacy skills. But does it not benefit both student and teacher to pay attention to developing writing skills that will help these students use writing more effectively to communicate their content knowledge? Students must understand that both their ideas and *how they communicate* those ideas are important. The assessment checklists in chapter 8 help address this issue. They are designed to give the greatest weight to the content knowledge demonstrated in the writing, but they do assess features of writing, such as organization style, and conventions.

HOW TO USE THIS BOOK

- Subject-area specialists and teachers who wish to integrate writing into subject areas will find chapter 2 helpful in establishing classroom routines and schedules for daily instruction and assessment. Later chapters provide suggestions for teaching and assessing content-area writing.

- Chapter 3 presents ideas and mini-lessons to assist students in searching for and selecting relevant information, taking notes, and organizing information.

- Chapters 4, 5, and 6 suggest ideas for teaching non-narrative writing, poetry, and narrative writing in content-area classes.

- Chapter 7 deals with writing conventions and presents suggestions for teaching spelling, punctuation, and grammar.

- Chapter 8 shows how to assess content-area writing and provides suggestions for conferencing with students to guide their revisions and editing.

- The final chapter looks at the difficulties some students have with writing and ways to help overcome them.

- The final section of the book contains a section of appendices with sample unit plans for teaching writing across the curriculum followed by a suggested list of further reading that will help address writing in content-areas such as science, social studies, music, art, health and physical education, and mathematics.

REFERENCES

Blake, B. E. *She Say, He Say: Urban Girls Write Their Lives.* Albany, NY: SUNY Press, 1997.

Brandt, D., and H. Graff. *Continuing the Conversation on Literacy Past, Present and Future.* NCTEAR Midwinter Conference. Columbus, OH: February, 2005.

Emig, J. "Hand, eye, brain: Some 'basics' in the writing process." In J. Emig, D. Goswami, and M. Butler (Eds.), *The Web of Meaning: Essays on Writing, Teaching, Learning and Thinking,* 109-121. Upper Montclair, NJ: Boynton/Cook Publishers, 1983.

Finders, M. J. *Just Girls: Hidden Literacies and Life in Junior High.* Urbana, IL: NCTE, 1997.

Lensmire, T. *When Children Write: Critical Re-visions of the Writing Workshop.* New York: Teachers College Press, 1994.

Murray, D. *Shop Talk: Learning to Write With Writers.* Portsmouth, NH: Heinemann, 1990.

Peterson, S. "Gender Meanings in Grade Eight Students' Talk About Classroom Narrative Writing." *Gender and Education,* 14(4), 351-366, 2003.

Wood Ray, K. *The Writing Workshop: Working Through the Hard Parts (and they're all hard parts).* Urbana, IL: NCTE, 2001.

CHAPTER 2

ORGANIZING CLASSROOMS FOR WRITING IN CONTENT AREAS

Take writers seriously.

Help writers to have high expectations and demonstrate that you have high expectations for yourself.

Show students how to write by writing yourself - you are learning alongside your students.

Give writers a chance to say something worthwhile.

(Donald Graves 1994, p.13)

FINDING A PLACE FOR WRITING IN CONTENT CLASSES

Think about the last science, social studies, health, music, art, or mathematics unit you taught. Were students involved in hands-on activities with concrete materials? Did they hear guest speakers? Did they go on field trips? Did they consult the Internet, books, magazines, newspapers, or other print sources and take notes on what they learned? Did they discuss problems or questions in small groups? Did they demonstrate their learning through creating a visual, oral, or written product? Did students learn how to improve their writing through mini-lessons and conferences with their teacher and peers? Most likely, you can answer "Yes!" to all these questions, except, perhaps, for the final one. In this chapter, plans and ways of organizing content classes will help provide support for students in their content learning as well as in their writing development.

When integrating writing into content areas, planning is complicated by juggling content-area objectives and writing objectives. A framework for integrating writing into the curriculum is a useful tool (see figure 2.1a). By using this framework, incorporating instruction of content area and developing students' writing abilities can both be addressed. Figure 2.1b is a template for you to use in your own unit planning. Examples that show how this planning framework might be used in science, social studies, and health classes are found in appendix A.

Framework for Integrating Writing Across the Curriculum

1. Identify the content-area learning objectives and the writing objectives that will serve as the centre for students' learning.

2. Develop activities to help students gather and organize the information that they have connected to the learning objectives. These activities can include concrete experiences, such as hands-on activities with manipulatives, experiments, interviews, reading print and non-print texts, drawing, painting, sculpting, fieldtrips—the possibilities are as vast as your imagination allows.

3. Provide choice for students as they select their writing formats, and encourage them to think about the content within the subject area. Introduce students to a range of formats that they can use for their writing. Be sure to include narrative, non-narrative, and poetry. These all work well for any content-area.

4. Allow time for students to interact with peers and to work independently to gather and organize information, write, revise and discover, edit, and communicate their learning to an audience.

5. Teach mini-lessons that address the original objectives and address the new objectives that arise as students engage in the learning experiences.

6. If possible, schedule time for one-on-one student-teacher conferences.

7. Determine how students will share their writing with a wider audience.

Figure 2.1a Framework for integrating writing across the curriculum

Integrating Writing in a Content-Area Unit

Integrating writing for a unit on: _____

Subject Area Concepts:

Writing Objectives:

Writing Activity:

Strategies for Gathering Information:

Mini-Lessons:

Resources for Gathering Information:

Figure 2.1b Template for integrating writing into content-area units

In your planning, the content objectives will likely come from the content-area curriculum you teach. The writing objectives and assessment criteria can come from both the language arts curriculum, and from previous assessments of students' writing. Focus the mini-lessons on elements of writing, such as using dialogue in fiction writing, supporting the main point with examples and details in non-narrative writing, or using specific words in poetry writing. Students may have demonstrated in their previous writing that they had difficulty with these elements, or the curriculum may indicate that these are important elements for students to master.

Leonora, a grade-eight science teacher, does not include a written project for every science unit. She usually selects a few science units each year that provide plenty of scope for students' writing. Students carry out writing projects during these units, but during the rest of the year, students' writing in science includes the more traditional note taking and short-answer writing. Leonora does, however, emphasize elements of good writing in her feedback and assessments of all the writing that students do in her science classes. By doing this, Leonora demonstrates that all teachers are writing teachers and that communicating effectively through writing is important in all subject areas, not just language arts.

When students are writing in any subject area, it is important to schedule writing time as often as possible during the week. If you are teaching language arts, as well as content areas, you can integrate the content writing assignments with the other writing in writers workshop. The mini-lessons, conferencing, and sharing of writing (in small groups, with a partner, or the whole class) can take place during language arts classes or content-area classes. The writing that you assign for content-area classes can be woven into the fabric of the writer's workshop. During the time allotted for writing, students can be working on their free-choice writing or on their content-area writing. They may need guidance in planning their time so that they can meet the deadlines for their content writing.

It is possible for a piece of writing from a content-area class to be only one of a number of pieces of writing that students complete during the term for their language arts/English grade. If writing is your focus, you might extend your writers workshops into new genres and topics by pulling information from content-area topics. The content-area classes can be used to help students gather information for their writing. Writers workshop can be used for both writing and writing instruction. The suggestions in this book then complement the work that you are already doing in writers workshop.

Integration of writing instruction and concepts can be challenging when you first start to contemplate writing across the curriculum. Scheduling is one area that demands great attention. In figure 2.2, content classes and language arts/English classes are scheduled from week one though six as unit plans. The figure shows how writing and concept instruction can be integrated. In this example, the teacher teaches language arts, mathematics, social studies, science, health, and art. Students have time for writing throughout the content-area unit of study and during writers workshop time in language arts.

For teachers who are subject specialists, figure 2.3 shows an example of scheduling writing into the content-area units. This schedule shows weeks one through six and outlines how to incorporate writing. Students write only in the subject-area classes.

Schedule for Teachers Who Teach Language Arts and Content Classes

	Content Classes	Language Arts/English Classes
Week One	• Students and teacher complete a K-W-L for the content topic. • Students read about the unit topic, discuss the topic in small groups. • Students do hands-on activities related to the content-area topic. • The teacher introduces the writing assignment and shows examples of the genre students will be using in their writing.	• Students carry out the activities for Week Six Content Classes in some of the writers workshop classes.
Weeks Two through Five	• Students continue reading about the topic. • Students continue doing hands-on activities related to the content-area topic. • The teacher devotes four or five 40-minute content-area classes to the writing assignment. • The teacher continues to conference with students and teaches mini-lessons to support students' writing.	• Students continue with their free-choice writing. • Students begin planning and gathering information and writing for the content-area writing assignment. • The teacher writes along with the students and teaches mini-lessons on the assigned genre for the content-area writing assignment.
Week Six	• Students continue to write, revise, and edit their writing. • Students complete their writing and read it to a partner, in a small group, or to the whole class. • The end product or published writing may be sent out to a more public audience. • The teacher celebrates and assesses the writing.	• Students use some writers workshop time for content-area writing and their free-choice writing. • The teacher continues to conference with students. • The teacher continues teaching mini-lessons to support students writing for content area and other writing.

Figure 2.2 Six-week unit planned by teacher who teaches language arts and content-area subjects

Schedule for Teachers Who Teach Content Classes Only

Unit Planned by a Subject-Area Specialist

Weeks One and Two

- Students read about the unit topic, discuss the topic in small groups, and do hands-on activities related to the content-area topic as they would in any content-area unit.

- The teacher introduces the writing assignment and shows how content topics can be incorporated into many genres.

- Students begin planning, gathering information through reading, and doing hands-on activities.

- Students write a first draft.

In some classes, 15-20 minutes are devoted to writing. In other classes, all of the time is used for reading, discussing, and hands-on activities.

Weeks Three through Five

- Students' continue reading about the topic and doing hands-on activities related to the content-area topic.

- Students continue planning, gathering information, and drafting their writing.

- The teacher continues to teach mini-lessons to support students' writing.

In some classes, 15-20 minutes are devoted to writing, conferencing, and so on. In others, 20-40 minutes are devoted to writing and writing instruction. There may be a few classes devoted entirely to reading and hands-on activities. During this time, students think about how the reading and activities can contribute to their writing. They may be doing some writing at home, as well.

Week Six

- Students continue to write, revise, and edit their writing.

- Students complete their writing and read it to a partner, in small groups, or to the whole class.

- Students' end product or published writing may be sent out to a more public audience.

- The teacher celebrates and assesses the writing.

Figure 2.3 Six-week unit planned by subject-area specialist

TOPICS AND TIME

In writers workshop, to truly get students to say something worthwhile in their writing, we open topic and genre possibilities to whatever students can imagine. Sometimes, however, assigning topics and genres will help students venture into new territory and try something that they would not try on their own. The same is true in content-area writing. The difference is that we provide students with a range of topics that are related to the content-area learning objectives. These allow students to extend and enrich their conceptual learning and also to demonstrate their learning through writing. Perhaps it is worth cautioning against assigning a very narrow topic (e.g., the life cycle of a mealworm), or dictating an opening sentence that all students must use in their writing (e.g., "Would you believe that your body size and shape are influenced by diet, exercise, and the size and shape of your parents and grandparents?). If we want the writing to be a tool for discovery and new learning, students should always have some choice in their writing. It will then be more worthwhile, it will say something, and it will be meaningful for the student.

Leslie is a grade-six science teacher. She asked her students to show what they had learned about levers and motion. They wrote using their choice of genre and came up with some creative and fulfilling product. Because she planned to use the students' writing in her assessment for a unit on motion, Leslie asked students to ensure that they include in their writing at least two of the nine concepts (e.g., motion, oscillating, linear motion, rotational motion, reciprocating motion, force, friction, fulcrum, and lever). Beyond that, students had full control of the topics and genres they used in their writing.

At other times the parameters for writing in the content areas may be placed on the genre, because it forces students to stretch beyond those genres that they gravitate toward and are most comfortable with. Making them stretch beyond their comfort can allow students to be more creative. Khaled is a grade-five social studies teacher. He assigned a persuasive letter on an issue that had arisen in a unit on First Nation peoples of North America. He wanted to introduce students to a type of writing that they rarely chose in their free-choice writing. In this case, the genre was determined by the teacher, but students had a wide range of topics within the content area from which to choose. All of these topics satisfied the learning outcomes.

Regardless of how narrowly defined the topic or genre for the writing, students need to become well informed about the topic, and they need some experience with the genre. No one can write from inside a vacuum. The types of activities that have long been associated with teaching in content classes –

working with concrete materials, field trips, interviews, reading print-based materials of all types, small-group discussions, and so on – provide the information. This means that the format of content classes does not have to change drastically when integrating writing.

You may need to help students determine the types of information that will be important and help them record that information so it can be used later in their writing. These skills, together with helping students organize the information will be the topics of mini-lessons. Chapter 3 presents numerous suggestions for supporting students in searching for, recording, and organizing information for their writing.

When incorporating writing into content classes, a new challenge will be to allot adequate time to support students in their writing. This includes time to complete mini-lessons on writing, time devoted to writing, and time for conferencing with the students. If a teacher is both a content-area teacher and a language arts teacher, time can be borrowed from writers workshop in language arts periods. If a teacher is exclusively a content-area teacher, some time has to be taken from other activities to devote to writing. Students will also likely have to do some writing at home, on their own time. Leonora found that her students enjoyed doing much of their writing at home. They often got feedback from their peers by e-mailing their emerging drafts to their peers or by reading what they had written over the phone. This kind of individual effort to communicate their writing was a welcome result of incorporating writing into the content area.

Students who have put a great deal of effort and time into their writing will want it to be read by a wider audience than just their teacher. Indeed, their motivation and commitment to writing will be much higher if they know that their writing is going to have an impact on someone else and will not simply be the source of a grade on their report card. It is important to plan opportunities for students to share the writing with others. The audience can be a small group of peers, the whole class, students in another class or school, or readers of a local newspaper. In one of my classes, for example, students created handbooks on caring for animals. Their handbooks were distributed to local veterinarian offices and became reading material for pet owners as they waited to have their pets attended to.

CLASSROOM ORGANIZATIONAL ISSUES

My experience with grades 4-8 students shows that they find the idea of writing in science, social studies, health, or any other subject area very appealing.

Students get excited at the thought of using stories, cartoons, letters, and so on to demonstrate their learning and to learn more about the topics. The challenge for their teacher is to organize the class so that students' interests are sustained and their writing is supported.

Graves (1994) tells us that "if children are to choose topics or figure out how they will solve writing problems, they need a highly predictable classroom" (p.111). A number of things should be predictable:

1. Students write regularly once a writing assignment is introduced.

2. There are certain routines to be followed to start each class. Students might begin by taking out their folders/notebooks/binders and reviewing what they have written so far.

    Students might use notebooks, folders, or binders to store the information they gather and to organize drafts of their writing. Because students may be collecting artifacts, newspaper clippings, and printouts from websites, folders or binders might be more practical than notebooks. I borrow from Camille Allen's (2001) suggestions to help students organize their notebooks/folders/binders. Students divide them into two sections. In the *Portfolio* section, students keep drafts of their writing. In the *Resources* section, students keep the computer printouts, notes they have taken while reading/viewing/interviewing, or any other sources of information they are planning to use for their writing.

3. There are routines for:

    *   getting supplies
    *   approaching a peer for assistance
    *   signalling to the teacher for help
    *   gathering information from books and magazines in the classroom or school library, or from the classroom or computer lab computers
    *   scheduling a student-teacher conference with the teacher
    *   determining how students will read their writing to a peer audience

Sharing writing in smaller groups works well if there are many students who want to share at the same time. If one student wants to read a very long piece, he/she might be given a time limit and instructions to summarize some parts and then read other parts to stay within the time limit.

4. Teacher and students negotiate noise levels, time for quiet writing, time for student-teacher conferences, and time for reading published writing to the class.

5. When students have finished a piece, they can start another one, or they can read or work on hands-on projects, computer work, or other work that will give them information or inspiration for writing another piece. They might also create multimedia presentations of their writing.

In addition, setting up the structures of process-writing classrooms (Calkins 1994; Graves 1994) can provide the predictability that students need. These structures involve students working with peers, either formally in author groups, or less formally in peer conferences. The teacher's role is to serve as a model, by writing alongside the students. Teachers also provide ongoing feedback on students' writing, either in formal student-teacher conferences or informally, in conversations while students are writing. When assigning due dates for drafts and final products and when planning mini-lessons, teachers respect students' unique writing processes, rather than expecting all students to plan on one day, draft the next day, revise the following day, and then edit the final day before handing in an assignment.

Author Groups

Students could meet formally with peers (two to four students per group) to provide feedback about each other's writing. In these groups, students and the teacher (when it is appropriate) read drafts of their own writing. Group members take turns describing characteristics of the writing that are effective, and they also explain what is unclear, confusing, or needs to be revised. The goal is to build students' confidence as writers and give them a sense of what impression their writing is making on their audience. Teachers may need to show students how to provide constructive suggestions to the writer. Students often feel vulnerable when reading their written work to peers, so it is important for teachers to establish expectations and model respectful ways to make suggestions within the author groups.

Peer Conferencing

If classrooms are set up so students can talk to one another while they write, they can then share their ideas with peers and use these ideas in their writing. They can also receive ongoing feedback about how clearly they communicate their ideas and about how their peers will accept their writing.

Teachers Provide Ongoing Feedback to Students

After teaching mini-lessons, you might schedule student-teacher conferences or walk around the classroom, responding to students' requests for assistance and reading students' writing as they compose. I usually schedule no more than one or two conferences in any 40-minute period. During these teacher-student conversations of about 5–10 minutes, I usually ask students what they want feedback on, and then also comment on more obvious aspects of the writing that strike me as strong or as needing to be revised or edited. Sometimes, I concentrate on specific aspects that have been addressed in mini-lessons. Chapter 8 provides further suggestions for providing feedback to students.

Teachers Write with Students

Teachers show the value of writing by sharing the same joys and challenges as they write alongside their students. Students will see that even though adults, sometimes get frustrated with the writing process, their teacher for instance, they still see writing as important and rewarding. Often, in the first ten minutes of a writing class, I write at the overhead projector so that students can see my evolving writing and I can still monitor what they are doing.

Recognizing Students' Personal Writing Processes

Any writing model is a presentation of *a* writing process, rather than *the* writing process. Often, writers engage in some form of planning and thinking through of ideas prior to writing, either in the writer's head or on paper, through brainstorming, or by making wish lists, and so on. They do some initial drafts and further revisions of the writing, and finally some editing before publication. These processes do not look the same for every writer, nor do they occur in the same order for every writer. We must respect the idiosyncratic nature of writing and be open to each students' specific needs for help with planning, drafting, revising, and editing at various stages as they work toward a satisfying written product.

REFERENCES

Calkins, L. *The Art of Teaching Writing 2nd Ed.* Portsmouth, NH: Heinemann, 1994.

Graves, D. *A Fresh Look at Writing.* Portsmouth, NH: Heinemann, 1994.

CHAPTER 3

SEEKING, RECORDING, AND ORGANIZING INFORMATION

> Today's students live in a world where increases in the amount of information being produced will continue to be exponential. . . They need to be savvy users of information. They need to know how information works and how information can work for them.
>
> **(Carol Koechlin and Sandi Zwaan 2001, p.6)**

THE INFORMATION SEARCH

The words of Carol Koechlin and Sandi Zwaan express what we all recognize – that an ever-expanding universe of information is available to our students. Our challenge is to nurture students' curiosity about the world and help them access the information in order to answer questions, solve problems, and imagine what could be.

For some students, accessing information from a variety of sources will be second nature. Others will need support using the Internet or online catalogue at their school or public libraries. Some may also need help finding appropriate books, articles, pamphlets, videos, and posters at their reading levels. We cannot assume that students know how to use the library's Dewey Decimal system (or whatever system the library uses). Furthermore, once students have books in their hands, we cannot assume that they know how to use the table of contents and the index to locate information. We need to seek out every opportunity to teach and reinforce these skills. Leonora, a grade-eight teacher, reinforces these skills every time she asks students to find a page in their science textbooks. Instead of directing them to a particular page, she gives students the topic and asks them to use the table of contents, the index, or headings and subheadings of chapters to find the correct page.

Students also need support in shaping the questions that will focus their information searches. They need help to identify relevant information, make connections between ideas, and organize the information into meaningful themes. This chapter is designed to provide a starting point for giving students the support they need.

Mini-Lessons: Seeking Information on the Internet

The Internet is an enormous and sometimes overwhelming resource for students seeking ideas and information for their content writing. Although a number of search engines are available, the one that most students and teachers use is *Google* (www.google.com). This popular website has actually developed its own language and has become a verb: "Why don't you try 'googling' that to find out more?" If students are looking for an alternative, they might try www.hotbot.com. *Hotbot* allows students to conduct advanced searches with a filter for finding key words in any position on a web page (e.g., in the title, in the URL, or in the body of the text). It allows students to filter their search by date. From *Hotbot,* students can also access *Google* and *Ask Jeeves,* which is a search engine that acts on specific questions.

Two skills are particularly important in being able to locate reliable information on the Internet and from other print and visual media sources: (1) searching using key words and (2) assessing the credibility of sources of information.

Activity 1: Key word searches

Demonstrations and guided pracatice are the best ways I know to support students in narrowing down search terms for information on the Internet or from other sources. This involves walking students through a search using a topic addressed in your content area or in the example in figure 3.1. This demonstration can be followed by guided practice in a whole-class or small-group lesson, as you help students narrow their focus to useful keywords for topics addressed in the unit of study. Guided practice then leads to independent practice as students conduct key word searches on their own for the topics they have selected for their writing.

Narrowing a Key Word Search

Topic: What do properties of air and principles of flight have to do with being able to fly in an airplane?

A search using these key words will yield the following hits:

properties air – 13,500,000 hits

properties air flight – 1,470,000 hits

"properties of air" airplane – 6,770 hits

"properties of air" "principles of flight" – 177 hits

In the final key word search, the number of hits (177) is still high, but the descriptions of the web sites show that the majority will provide useful information to answer the research question. Internet search engines list the sites from highest to lowest probability that you will find what you are looking for at the topic, given the search words you typed in. Generally, students will find something relevant in the first two pages of the list on any search engine, and will avoid any wild goose chases.

Tips for Searches:

1. Search engines ignore common words and characters such as "where" and "how," as well as certain single digits and single letters, because they tend to slow down a search without improving the results. It is not necessary to include "and" in the search, because the search engine assumes you want both terms included and not just one of them.

2. If a common word is essential to getting the results you want, you can include it by putting a space and then a " + " sign in front of it.

3. If you want to narrow the search to the most specific topic, use quotation marks around the phrase. This will only look for the exact words in the exact order you have typed them into the search engine.

Figure 3.1 Narrowing a key word search

Activity 2: Assessing the quality of information

Students need to recognize that not all the information on the Internet can be trusted or is accurate. Anyone can put information on a website, regardless of her/his motivation, credentials, depth of knowledge, or skill level. Intention and perspective of the creators should also be considered in books and other media, as well. Our students should be encouraged to determine the creator's or designer's purpose for creating print or visual media. They should assess the diversity of viewpoints presented and how thoroughly and thoughtfully the writers and producers have explained each perspective.

Students might not be aware that the presence or absence of particular information may be deliberate. Attention or inattention to perspectives and unconscious assumptions about the topic can sometimes lead a writer in narrow directions. In addition to fostering students' awareness of the creator/ designer's underlying assumptions, we might also need to help students recognize stereotypes that present unwarranted biases toward certain groups of people and values.

Assessing the quality of information also includes determining the depth of knowledge that authors and designers bring to their writing and visual creations. Students should look at the number of sources consulted by the creator/designer and determine how recently the information was reported. Population numbers or information about scientific discoveries quickly become outdated, for example.

As a general rule, it is best to read a number of sources on a topic, and not just rely on one (e.g., the Internet). Students can then compare and contrast the information of various sources and determine which facts and ideas appear most frequently. They should also look up information on the sources of the information to determine the contributor's level of expertise. More experienced researchers can look at the references the creator/designer consult in their own information gathering. This will show how widely they sought out their information and help determine how trusted their information can be.

In teaching students to judge the quality of sources, you may demonstrate strategies for using Internet, print, and visual media on topics of study in content-area classes. Students may find figure 3.2 helpful when they are searching for information.

How Accurate Is the Internet Information?

Use these questions to help you decide what information you can trust and what information you should ignore.

1. What viewpoint does the information source seem to promote?

2. What different viewpoints are presented? Does the website creator/designer fairly present each one?

3. What information seems to be missing? Whose viewpoints seem to be missing?

4. Are there any stereotypes? What are they? Why do you think the creator/designer used stereotypes?

5. What information seems to be exaggerated (e.g., "Never before has anyone tried ...) or overgeneralized (e.g., Everyone knows that ...)?

6. What credentials does the creator/designer have to make her/him an expert on the topic?

7. What sources did the creator/designer consult to make him/her more knowledgeable?

8. Is the information up to date?

9. Does the creator/designer present opinions as facts? (e.g., "It is well known that ...")

10. When you compare the information from three or four different sources, what contradictions do you find? How will you decide which information to use if there are contradictions?

Figure 3.2 Determining validity of Internet information

Activity 3: Developing questions for interviews

The interview is a helpful tool for gathering firsthand information from people. It can be an excellent alternative to accessing information in print, electronic, or visual form. Developing interview questions is difficult for students of all ages. Understanding what information students are seeking will help them define how to best develop their questions. Questions need to be created in

Asking Good Interview Questions

Directions: Ask the two questions below after each interview question.

1. Is the question open-ended enough so that the interviewee can give lots of information, or is it a closed-ended, yes/no question?

2. Does the question clearly relate to the overall topic of the interview?

If you answer "no" to either of these questions, revise the question so it is open-ended and related to the topic.

Then, talk with a partner about what you have learned about how to create good interview questions.

INTERVIEW QUESTIONS
**Topic: What do people think they should do, and
what do they actually do to stay healthy?**

1. What physical activities do you do every day to stay healthy? What do you do just once or twice a week?

2. Do you like junk food?

3. Would you ever start smoking? Why or why not?

4. How much television do you watch on week days?

5. Do you think people should eat vegetables and fruit every day?

6. Are you worried about your weight?

7. What are you trying to do to live a healthier life?

Figure 3.3 Asking good interview questions

such a way as to help the interviewee focus her/his response on the desired topic. One of the more difficult concepts for students to understand is the difference between open-ended and closed questions.

In this activity, students explore how to make questions clearly understandable so the interviewee knows what kind of information to provide and how to ask questions that give interviewees some room to respond (see figure 3.3). Following this activity, students are able to draw up a list of considerations for developing interview questions, and they create their own interview questions.

Mini-Lessons: Recording Information

Activity 1: Selecting relevant information

In an effort not to overlook important details, students often write down more information than they need when taking notes. The end result is a page of notes that looks suspiciously similar to the original information source. For most students, developing the skill of selecting only relevant information will likely require a great deal of modelling and guided support. Encourage students to think about the following questions as they read a book, magazine, pamphlet, or website about their topic:

- What kinds of information do you hope to find?

- What kinds of information do you expect to find as you read the headings?

- What information directly answers your questions?

- What information is interesting but doesn't really answer your questions?

Demonstrating what is relevant information in a source introduces students to different ways of thinking when taking notes. You might use figure 3.4 for one demonstration. In this example, the note taker highlights the parts of the text that are useful in answering a specific question about glaciers and explains why she thinks this information is relevant.

Deciding What Is Relevant

Information from the book, *Icebergs and Glaciers,* by Seymour Simon (unpaged)	My thoughts about what is relevant to my question.
Question: What causes glaciers to move?	I'm looking for information about the causes of movement.
In the early part of the twentieth century, Swiss and Italian scientists drilled holes straight down through the thickness of a glacier. Then they placed iron rods in the holes. Over the years, the scientists found that the rods bent at the top. This showed that the ice at the top of a glacier moves more quickly than the ice at the bottom.	This is interesting, but it explains which part of the glacier moves more quickly, not what causes glaciers to move.
The thicker the glacier the faster it moves. That's because the greater weight of the glacier causes the crystals of ice to creep more rapidly. Also, a steep glacier will flow much more quickly than one on level land.	The parts I've highlighted explain that thickness of the glacier, the slope of the land the glacier is on, and the temperature of the glacier cause its movement.
Temperature is a third factor that affects the speed of a glacier. The warmer the glacier the faster the ice moves, because there is a greater amount of meltwater beneath the ice. In fact, scientists sometimes group glaciers together depending upon whether they are cold or warm. But even "warm" glaciers are still freezing.	This part provides additional information about warm and cold glaciers, but doesn't explain what causes glaciers to move.

Figure 3.4 Deciding what is relevant

Activity 2: Three forms of note taking

1. Using sentence stems

Wray and Rospigliosi (1994) used this framework successfully to help students write notes in their own words. I modified their work by adding sentence stems that help students focus on what they are learning as they read, view, observe, or experience new ideas and information.

I learned that _____.

I will show readers how _____.

My readers will need to know that _____.

I need to find out more about _____.

Figure 3.5 can be copied for students to use or you may ask students to write the stems that work best for their notes. The sample in figure 3.6 demonstrates how students can use the template. This example is not complete, as the student still has additional information to locate and some discrepant information to verify.

Because students are completing sentence stems, their notes will take the form of sentences. If you prefer that students take notes in the form of key words and phrases, the next two frameworks (figure 3.7 and 3.8), may be more appropriate.

Note Taking: Completing Sentence Stems

Topic: _____

Sources Used: _____

I learned that:

I will show readers how:

My readers will need to know that:

I need to look for more information about:

Figure 3.5 Note taking: completing sentence stems

Note Taking: Completing Sentence Stems
An Example

Topic: What the Underground Railroad was and how it helped slaves from the southern US states

Sources Used:
Sadlier, R. *The Kids Book of Black Canadian History.* Toronto, ON: Kids Can Press, 2003.

Public Broadcasting System web site:
www.pbs.org/wgbh/aia/part4/4p2944.html

I learned that:
* Harriet Tubman was a slave who escaped from a plantation to St. Catharines, in 1850.
* songs like Swing Low, Sweet Chariot, Brother Moses Gone to de Promised Land, and Follow the Drinkin' Gourd gave directions on how to escape slavery to get to the northern states or to Canada

I will show readers how:
* the runaway slaves were helped by some white people and by freed slaves in the Underground Railroad. They called the places where runaway slaves would rest and eat "stations" and "depots." The people who helped were called "stationmasters" and "conductors."

My readers will need to know that:
* Congress passed a Fugitive Slave Law to help Southern slave owners to bring back escaping slaves.
* The Quakers were part of the Underground Railroad. They raised money to buy clothes, feed the escaping slaves, and pay for boat and train rides.

I need to look for more information about:
* other conductors on the Underground Railroad: John Fairfield in Ohio, the son of a slaveholding family and Levi Coffin, a Quaker, who assisted more than 3,000 slaves
* how many people Harriet Tubman freed. One source says 300 and another says 750.
* when the Underground Railroad started. One source says 1831 when Nat Turner revolted against slavery and the other says 1810.

Figure 3.6 Note taking using sentence stems: An example

2. Notes and thoughts

This form of note taking is valuable because it encourages students to think deeply about information as they take notes. It is both a note-taking form and a forum for exploratory writing. Students take notes in point form and then reflect on what the information means to them. They draw on previous experiences and background knowledge, and may bring in other information that they learn through asking a peer or their teacher, or by consulting a dictionary. The format provides space for wondering, hypothesizing, and planning what students might try in the future. A template for students is found in figure 3.7. A good example of one student's use of the *Notes and Thoughts* format can be found in figure 3.8.

Notes and Thoughts

Topic: _____

Sources: _____

_____

Notes	Thoughts

Figure 3.7 Notes and thoughts template

Notes and Thoughts
An Example

Topic: How do percussion instruments make sounds?

Sources: www.cafemuse.com/soundgarden/makingmusic/percussion.htm
www.scott.k12.va.us/bmoorehouse/percussion.htm

Notes	Thoughts
Part or all of the percussion instruments vibrate when they are struck, shaken, or scraped	I know that sound is made of vibrations. I wonder if almost anything could be a percussion instrument if all you have to do is hit, shake, or scrape it. I'd like to try making different kinds of percussion instruments.
Types: melodic (plays melodies — like a vibraphone) and non-melodic (makes sounds that don't change in pitch)	I usually think of drums and shakers as being percussion instruments, but I didn't know that instruments like xylophones that play melodies were percussion instruments. All you do is hit them to make them vibrate, so I guess that makes them a percussion instrument.
Two parts: Primary Vibrator — the part that creates sound (e.g., snare drum -- membrane stretched across the metal frame) Resonant Vibrator makes the sound louder (e.g., snare drum — the metal case)	It makes sense that the part you hit or scrape or that gets something shaken against it would be the primary vibrator — that's what makes the sound. I looked up the word *resonance*. It means that something continues to sound and the sound is deep and full. That must mean that if you didn't have the resonant vibrator, the instrument would not be very loud and the sound would end quickly.

Figure 3.8 Notes and thoughts: An example

3. Cornell note-taking framework

Taking notes is made easier when students use this chart to make connections between their questions and the information they find about the topic. The analysis section at the bottom encourages students to make connections and reflect on what the notes mean to them. As students begin to write, this analysis allows for some exploratory thinking about the topic.

Before allowing students to take notes independently, show them the framework example in figure 3.10 and then give them a copy of figure 3.9, the Cornell note-taking frame (based on the work of Pauk 1974), to take notes independently. You might want to make an overhead transparency of figure 3.10. A discussion of how one student has used it to take notes from Linda Granfield's *Where Poppies Grow* will show one way that students can use the frame. The student can be looking up further information to answer new questions in the "Questions" column (see parentheses).

Taking Notes Using the Cornell Framework

Topic: _____

Sources Used: _____

_____

Questions	Notes

Short Summary of Notes:

Enlarge on the photocopier at 121%.

Figure 3.9   Cornell note-taking framework

Taking Notes Using the Cornell Note-taking Framework: An Example

Topic: World War I

Sources Used: Granfield, Linda. *Where Poppies Grow: A World War I Companion.* Markham, ON: Fitzhenry and Whiteside, 2001.

Questions	Notes
How and when did WWI start? (unanswered question: What countries besides Belgium, France and Canada fought with Britain?)	• Started in August, 1914 after heir to Austro-Hungarian throne was murdered in June, 1914 • Germany invaded Belgium. Britain had to defend Belgians because of a treaty.
Where was the war fought? (unanswered question: What year did the US join the Allies?)	• in Belgium (e.g., Mons, Ypres) and France (e.g., Vimy, the Somme) • in trenches — three lines, the front line closest to the enemy, the support line and the reserve line • at sea — German U-boats (submarines) sank supply ships from North America (brought US into war) • by air — dirigibles (e.g., German Zeppelin) and planes dropped bombs

Short Summary of Notes

Britain and her allies fought the Germans in Belgium and France after the German army invaded Belgium in 1914. Most of the fighting took place from trenches dug in places like Ypres and the Somme, but planes and dirigibles also dropped bombs. The Germans tried to stop supplies coming from North America by blowing up supply ships on their way to Britain. This brought the Americans into the war.

Figure 3.10 Cornell note-taking framework: An example

Mini-Lessons: Organizing Information

Activity 1: K-W-L

Donna Ogle (1986) introduced teachers to K-W-L, a structure for gathering information that has become ubiquitous in classrooms. Students assess what they *know* (K) about a topic, ask questions about *what* (W) they want to learn, and then read/view/observe/survey/interview to *learn* (L) more about that topic. This format helps students think about specific types of information they should search for in preparation for their writing. The questions help students organize the information they gather. The information can be made into headings and subheadings for students' writing. Figure 3.11 is a template that can be used by students to organize their information in a K-W-L format.

K-W-L: Note Taking and Organizing Information

Topic _____

Sources: _____

_____

K What I know about the topic	W What I want to learn about the topic	L What I learned about the topic

Figure 3.11 K-W-L frame

Activity 2: Using compare/contrast charts

When a writing task requires students to compare and contrast two ideas, people, or things, using a compare/contrast format for taking notes helps organize the information. A template for students' use is found in figure 3.12. As shown in figure 3.13, two students took notes on the differences between the two ideas/people/things. The students also identified the common points. After identifying how the student took notes to compare and contrast two key figures of Canadian Confederation, they can read the poem that the writer composed (see chapter 5, page 80) to see how the students used notes in their poem for two voices.

Compare/Contrast Chart

Overall Topic: _____

Differences

Similarities

Figure 3.12 Compare/contrast chart

Compare/Contrast Chart:
An Example

Overall Topic: Key individuals and events leading to Canadian confederation

Differences

Sir George-Étienne Cartier	Sir John A. Macdonald
• worked for French-Canadian interests within British parliamentary system	• Tory supporter who favored business and railways and Anglican Church. Loyal to British
• elected to the legislature as a Canada East member when 29 years old	• first elected to legislature in 1844
• supported the 1837-1838 rebellion in Lower Canada and fled to the United States to avoid prison	• persuaded Liberals and Bleus to join to form the Liberal-Conservative Party in 1856
• leader of Le Parti Bleu	• wrote most of the 72 Resolutions of the British North between French and America Act. Presented these at the English Quebec Conference in 1864
• saw the new federation as a way of promoting better understanding	• chaired the London Conference in 1866

Similarities

• The Great Coalition with Cartier, Brown and Macdonald was formed in 1864 ending coalition governments that lasted months or days

• They both spoke at the Charlottetown meeting in 1864 about a federal system of government

• They both supported Confederation at the Quebec Conference in 1864

Figure 3.13 Compare/contrast chart: One example

Activity 3: Developing outlines

Outlines give students a global sense of the information they have gathered and make clear the connections among the ideas. A good outline gives students a clearer idea of where they will be moving with their writing. Without an outline, students may become confused and may try to include too little or too much information in their writing. In the writing process, however, students should not be expected to follow their outlines to the letter. New ideas arise as students write and gather information, and new directions emerge for their writing. To some extent, encourage students to stray from the outline to allow for deeper understandings. We would be disappointed if students' thinking was the same at the end of their writing as it had been when they created their outlines. Even so, the process of developing an outline is still necessary and should be encouraged.

In this activity, students begin by reading their notes and thoughts (see figure 3.14a) and circling the ideas that fit together. They might cut them out and paste them together (physically or on the computer), as the student did in figure 3.14b. Once they have all the similar ideas together, they can then think about what all the related ideas are saying and come up with the big ideas or themes. Have the students write the emerging themes as headings for each category, in the same way the students did in figure 3.14b. Formal outlines using Roman numerals and other numbering systems are not necessary. Students organize their notes and find connections between the examples and the supporting details, and cluster them together under appropriate descriptive headings. From their outline with the headings and supporting information, students can readily begin to write.

Notes and Thoughts

Topic: Alexander Graham Bell and His Inventions
Sources: MacLeod, E. *Alexander Graham Bell: An Inventive Life*. Toronto: Kids Can Press, 1999. • www.pbs.org/wgbh/amex/telephone/peopleevents/mabell.html

Notes	Thoughts
• born in Edinburgh, Scotland in 1847	He was 23 years old when he moved with his family.
• Both brothers died of tuberculosis and AGB was sick, so family moved to Ontario in 1870	
• His father created Visible Speech — symbols to help hearing-impaired communicate	His father was interested in sounds, too.
• AGB taught at Boston University as professor of Vocal Physiology and Elocution	He was inventing all the time and had a job as a professor. I wonder if he had time for any fun.
• As a child — experimented with system to collect rainwater and pipe it to the bathroom — his family had a shower	
• Tried to make a telegraph that could carry more than one message at a time	I wonder what I would say if I was having the first phone conversation. I think the people sang for 3 hours or something. I guess that's a good idea.
• Noticed that sound could make a metal disk vibrate — realized that sound could change electric currents	
• Used a transmitter in offices in Brantford and Paris, Ontario, to send voice messages over the Dominion Telegraph Company lines	
• Married Mabel Hubbard, his deaf student in 1877. They had two daughters.	If AGB had lost the court case, I wouldn't be writing this report!
• AGB had to fight 15 years in court to keep patent rights to telephone. Others said they invented it first and he stole their ideas. AGB won.	
• AGB invented telephone probe to find bullet and save US President James Garfield when he was shot in 1881. The probe didn't save his life, but did save lives during WWI.	He seemed to be curious about everything and trying to fix lots of problems.
• invented audiometer, a device for testing hearing	
• invented an air conditioning system	
• invented distilling devices for turning seawater into drinking water	It would have been fun to be his kids. They could fly and skim along the water in his inventions.
• invented tetrahedral kites to fly carrying people	
• worked with Aerial Experiment Association to design a plane, Silver Dart, that flew in 1909 (first plane to fly in Canada), after the Wright brothers flew their plane in 1903	
• built a hydrofoil (boat travels over top of water). His "hydrodome" set a speed record of 112 km/h in 1919.	That's a cool thing to do to honor AGB.
• AGB died in 1922 at 75 years old. Telephone service stopped for one minute across N. America for his funeral.	

Figure 3.14a Notes and thoughts

Organizing Notes and Thoughts about AGB

AGB's Life with his Family
- born in Edinburgh, Scotland in 1847
- As a child — experimented with system to collect rainwater and pipe it to the bathroom — his family had a shower
- Both brothers died of tuberculosis and AGB was sick, so family moved to Ontario in 1870
- His father created Visible Speech — symbols to help hearing-impaired communicate
- AGB taught at Boston University as professor of Vocal Physiology and Elocution
- Married Mabel Hubbard, his deaf student in 1877. They had two daughters.

Inventing the Telephone
- Tried to make a telegraph that could carry more than one message at a time
- Noticed that sound could make a metal disk vibrate — realized that sound could change electric currents
- Used a transmitter in offices in Brantford and Paris, Ontario to send voice messages over the Dominion Telegraph Company lines.
- AGB had to fight 15 years in court to keep patent rights to telephone. Others said they invented it first and he stole their ideas. AGB won.
- AGB died in 1922 at 75 years old. Telephone service stopped for one minute across N. America for his funeral.

Other Inventions
- AGB invented telephone probe to find bullet and save US President James Garfield when he was shot in 1881. The probe didn't save his life, but did save lives during WWI.
- invented audiometer, a device for testing hearing
- invented an air conditioning system
- invented distilling devices for turning seawater into drinking water
- invented tetrahedral kites to fly carrying people
- worked with Aerial Experiment Association to design a plane, Silver Dart, that flew in 1909 (first plane to fly in Canada), after the Wright brothers flew their plane in 1903.
- built a hydrofoil (boat travels over top of water). His "hydrodome" set a speed record of 112 km/h in 1919.

Figure 3.14b Organizing notes and thoughts about Alexander Graham Bell

REFERENCES

Koechlin, C., and S. Zwaan. *Info Tasks for Successful Learning: Building Skills in Reading, Writing, and Research.* Markham, ON: Pembroke, 2001.

Ogle, D. "K-W-L: A Teaching Model that Develops Active Reading of Expository Text." *The Reading Teacher*, 39, 563-570, 1986.

Pauk, W. *How to Study in College.* Boston, MA: Houghton Mifflin, 1974.

Lewis, M., D. Wray, and P. Rospigliosi "…And I want it in your own words." *The Reading Teacher, 47(7),* 528-536, 1994.

Children and Young Adult Books

Granfield, L. *Where Poppies Grow: A World War I Companion.* Markham, ON: Fitzhenry and Whiteside, 2001.

MacLeod, E. *Alexander Graham Bell: An Inventive Life.* Toronto, ON: Kids Can Press, 1999.

Sadlier, R. *The Kids Book of Black Canadian History.* Toronto, ON: Kids Can Press, 2003.

Simon, S. *Icebergs and Glaciers.* New York, NY: William Morrow and Company, 1987.

CHAPTER 4

WRITING USING NON-NARRATIVE FORMS ACROSS THE CURRICULUM

The essay is a literary device for saying almost everything about almost anything.

(Aldous Huxley in Robertson 1997, p.223)

WHY WRITE NON-NARRATIVE IN CONTENT AREAS?

When we speak of teaching writing, we are usually referring to narrative writing. I use the term non-narrative instead of nonfiction because I am focusing on the form, rather than whether the content is factual or imagined. In most cases, narrative writing seems to overshadow other types of writing in elementary classrooms. You will likely find more narrative than non-narrative writing in students' portfolios and on display in school hallways. Lists of teaching resources are composed mainly of narrative writing, rather than non-narrative writing. With this is mind, narrative seems to be viewed as the genre of greater choice – like a fine box of chocolates. Non-narrative seems to be viewed as the genre of necessity – like a sack of potatoes.

Yet, the "chocolate side" of non-narrative is evident to writers like Aldous Huxley. In the quote that opens this chapter, he sees enormous scope in writing using the non-narrative essay. According to Huxley, students can write about any topic of their choice, saying whatever is important to them using non-narrative forms. Students have a multitude of choices in determining which form will best suit their intended purpose (see page 44). The broad range of topics and forms makes non-narrative a type of writing that is "most likely to spur children's passion and wonder for learning" (Harvey 2002, 12). I have observed students glued to the Internet or to magazines, willing to invest time and energy outside of class in their desire to learn more about a topic and communicate that learning using non-narrative genres. Many reluctant readers and writers, boys and girls, choose non-narrative in their reading and writing outside of school (Booth 2002).

In spite of the wide range of opportunities for communicating information and many students' obvious interest in non-narrative, researchers like Suzanne Hidi and Angela Hildyard (1983) found that adolescents have less control of non-narrative forms of writing than they do of narrative forms. They questioned whether non-narrative is inherently more difficult to write or whether students had less experience in writing non-narrative in the early grades of their schooling.

My hunch is that the latter is true. There is ample evidence that non-narrative writing is as natural as narrative writing. Marie Clay (1975) found that spontaneous writing of five-year old children took the form of lists of the letters, numbers, and words that they knew. Grade-one students wrote "All about" books, a list-like collection of facts, features, and attributes of the subject, along with writing personal narratives in Susan Sowers' class (Sowers 1985). We know pre-school children can communicate ideas in non-narrative format when they talk. Among the many ways they use language, young children ask questions, tell us about things they have seen, and direct us on what they want us to do. They do not only tell stories. More and more often, researchers are finding that narrative is not the only way that young children represent their worlds (Kamberelis 1999).

I present suggestions in this chapter for non-narrative writing across the curriculum. In addition to lists of non-narrative forms that students might choose in their writing, you will find ideas for helping students recognize what particular non-narrative forms can help them achieve.

IDEAS FOR WRITING NON-NARRATIVE ACROSS THE CURRICULUM

Social Studies

- Write a diary or blog of someone who lived during a period of time covered in the curriculum.

- Write a persuasive essay on a controversial current issue.

Science

- Write a script for an interview with certain organisms (or a "This Is Your Life" type television show), showing their life cycles.

- Design an advertisement for a model solar heating device designed and constructed by students.

Mathematics

- Write an explanation for carrying out a particular operation.

- Design a survey, carry out the survey, and record the results on a labelled graph/table.

Art

- Design a poster with both a visual design and text with student-created fonts to advertise a sculpture that students have created.

- Write a review of a favourite artist's work, using students' understanding of line, shape, form, texture, and colour.

Health

- Write an advice column on interpersonal relationships or healthy eating topics in the curriculum.

- Write instructions on how to give basic first aid.

Music

- Create a glossary of music terms that the student has learned.

- Create a PowerPoint presentation that describes and contains excerpts of music from a particular historical era (e.g., Renaissance, Baroque, Classical, Romantic).

NON-NARRATIVE, NON-POETIC FORMS: A SHORT LIST

We write to achieve particular purposes. We write to come to know ourselves and answer questions about our world. We are hopeful that we build relationships with our readers and that readers enjoy our writing. Additionally, we tend to use non-narrative forms for three functions: to persuade, to inform/explain, and to instruct/direct. The use of language in our world involves these purposes (Halliday 1975).

Often, a particular non-narrative form may serve more than one purpose, so classifying the forms according to purpose is difficult. The following chart (figure 4.0) shows some forms of writing that appear in different categories that serve more than one purpose. The other forms of writing are categorized according to their primary functions.

Non-Narrative Forms: A Short List

Forms that Persuade	Forms That Inform/Explain	Forms That Instruct/Direct
book reviews	book reviews	directions
advertisements	summaries	web pages
web pages	reports	instructions
persuasive essays	web pages	explanations
PowerPoint presentations	memos	PowerPoint presentations
blogs	interview scripts	advice columns
written debates	documentaries (video or audio)	blogs
commentaries	case studies	recipes
editorials	PowerPoint presentations	manuals
advice columns	monographs	procedures
letters	radio or television newscasts	posters
posters	letters	rules
want ads	newspaper articles	

Figure 4.0 Non-narrative forms: A short list

HELPING STUDENTS BECOME BETTER NON-NARRATIVE WRITERS AND LEARN CONTENT KNOWLEDGE

Mini-Lessons: Getting to Know the Possibilities and Demands of Genres

Activity 1: Introducing a variety of genres

The best way I have found for introducing non-narrative writing is to read various genres. In this way, students come to see that any number of genres can be used to communicate the information in their content-area subjects. A list of books, organized by subject area, is found in appendix B.

The challenge for students is to learn how each genre is structured to accomplish particular purposes. We do not want students to see genres as rigid sets of organizational structures. Instead, we want to show students that the non-narrative genres' structures are ever-evolving. They change to fit the contexts in which they are used. The most important thing about non-narrative genres is that writers can use them for their own purposes. I recommend finding as many examples as possible of particular genres for students to read, pointing out the similarities and differences in how the writers have adapted the non-narrative genre structures for their own purposes.

When you read to students, you might ask questions such as those in Figure 4.1.

Questions For Considering What Various Genres Have to Offer and What Formats They Use

1. What did you learn about _____ (topic)?

2. Show the paragraphs, sentences, lines, or words that give information about the topic.

3. How did the writer communicate the information in this type of text (genre)?

4. What makes this genre different from a story? From a poem?

5. How is this example of a _____ (whatever the genre is) similar to and how is it different from this other example?

6. What advice would you give to someone who is about to write using this genre?

Figure 4.1 Questions for considering what genres offer and what formats they use

After thinking about the structure of the genre and the ways in which writers can use the genre to communicate information, students have a starting point for their own writing. The next three activities narrow students' focus on features of three types of non-narrative writing.

Activity 2: Identifying features of non-narrative that informs

The list of non-narrative forms that provide information is lengthy. Generally, when we think of non-narrative forms, we think of those that inform (e.g., reports, summaries, documentaries, memos, newspaper articles, catalogues, radio or television news reports, websites). Our students read and listen to these and other non-narrative texts daily. Many students internalize features of texts that inform and can readily use these genres in their content-area writing. Other students need support in recognizing and using texts that inform. This activity asks students to compare and contrast two types of writing that inform: a newspaper article (see figure 4.2) and a report (see figure 4.3). Both deal with the same topic, simple machines. Students can use the chart in figure 4.4 to guide their analysis of the two non-narrative texts.

Students will likely note that non-narrative text intended to inform tends to have a main idea-detail structure. The writer states or implies the key ideas she/he is trying to convey and then provides specific, detailed information to elaborate on the main ideas. Headings and subheadings are often used, depending on the type of non-narrative text, to help readers identify the key ideas. The title is usually very descriptive and conveys the text's overall idea.

Students can use the information gathered from reading either the two student-written texts below or others from their lives to write non-narrative texts that inform readers about the topic in your content area.

Pulleys Used to Rescue Stranded Whales

There was a large commotion last week at the coast near the town of Fake Lake. A large group of whales had been stranded on the shores of the lake.

This presented a problem of not enough space for patrons seeking an afternoon of fun in the sun. The bigger problem was that the rescue team had to return the whales to the water before they died.

They tried every idea that came to their mind, including pushing the whale with a tractor and offering the whale $50.00 to just get up and swim back into the water. All failed miserably. Time was running out when Pat Mercury, a concerned passer-by, proposed that they implement a pulley system to lift and carry the whales to safety. Pat explained that a construction crane would do the work because cranes are designed to lift large amounts of weight.

The rescue workers hooked the whales and raised them one-by-one. They positioned the whales above a safe amount of water, lowered them into the water and detached the hoist. The whales were saved! The rescue team was befuddled as to why they did not think of this earlier. If it were not for a knowledgeable stranger's assistance, the whales would surely have perished. With that in mind, the members of the rescue team resigned, sure that staying on duty would hurt more than help.

Figure 4.2 Newspaper article

Levers for Dummies

What is a lever?

A lever is a simple machine. It consists of a rigid bar pivoted on a fixed point. A lever is used to transmit force, as in raising or moving a weight at one end by pushing down on the other.

How to use a lever!

The lever is used for prying or lifting. There are three main parts to a lever. One part of a lever is a fulcrum. A fulcrum is known as the point on which the bar rests. The fulcrum lies between the effort and the load. Now, what is the effort arm? The part of the lever between the effort and the fulcrum is the effort arm. The part of the lever between the fulcrum and the load is the load arm.

First class lever

Levers, in which the fulcrum is located between the effort and the load, are known as first class levers. An example of a first class lever is a see-saw.

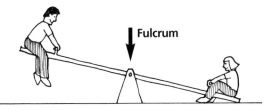

Second class lever

When the fulcrum is located at one end of the lever with the effort applied at the other end and the load in between, it is called a second class lever. Examples of a second class lever are a wheelbarrow and a nutcracker.

Third class lever

The final possibility of a lever is known as a third class lever. The effort is applied between the fulcrum and the load. An example of a third class lever are tongs.

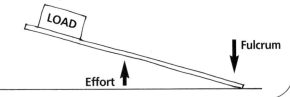

Figure 4.3 Report on levers

Looking at Informational Writing

Title	Overall idea What is it? How did the writer communicate this idea?	Key ideas What are they? How did you find the key ideas?	Supporting information What are the supporting details? How did the writer organize the writing to include supporting details?

Figure 4.4 Looking at informational writing

Activity 3: Identifying features of non-narrative forms that persuade

Young people often present an opinion with more than adequate emotional investment about some topics. For example, they should be allowed to go to a friend's party – their lives will be ruined or the world as they know it will end. Writing persuasively about topics in various content areas requires more than emotional investment, however. Students need a wider repertoire of tools for content-area persuasive writing.

Reading and analyzing examples of persuasive writing (e.g., letters to the editor, editorials, advice columns, blogs, advertisements, commentaries, book reviews) help to develop a sense of what writers can achieve through these non-narrative texts. The writing samples in figure 4.5 (blog on mathematics topic) and figure 4.6 (persuasive essay on art topic) are useful for demonstrating persuasive writing possibilities. Students might comment on what they have learned from the two persuasive pieces and what further information they would like writers to include. They might also discuss the level of interest that the writers have generated in their writing and how they have made their writing interesting. Students completing the chart in figure 4.7 will notice the following characteristics of persuasive writing:

- The writer states her/his position somewhere in the introduction (perhaps in the title) and again at the end.

- The writer states at least one reason why she/he has taken this position.

- The writer provides at least one reason why others might oppose his/her position and refutes the reason(s).

When students write their own persuasive papers on topics that relate to their daily lives, they can draw on their analysis of the two samples and of other persuasive writing.

Estimating in Math Is a Good Thing

My teachers told me that if I didn't estimate, I wouldn't be able to check to see if my answers made sense. **I didn't listen to them.** 😕 I used to think that estimating was a <u>waste of time</u>. I did my math questions as fast as I could so I wouldn't have homework. Who needs to round off big numbers to the nearest 10, 100, 1000, 10,000 and so on, and then add, multiply, subtract, or divide? Up until grade five, I didn't.

Then, in grade five, I had to do three pages of multiplication of two-digit by two-digit numbers and some of them were decimal numbers. **I got almost all of them wrong!!!?** 😲 I put the decimals in the wrong places!!? My teacher told me that if I had estimated first, I would have known that the decimals were in the wrong places. I learned the hard way that <u>estimating is worth the little bit of time it takes</u>. Rounding numbers and figuring out whether the answer should be closer to 2000 than to 20 saves the horror of getting your work back with a whole bunch of X's on it. Believe me. **Estimating is a good thing!** 😊

Figure 4.5   Student's persuasive writing in a blog

Let's Keep Art

You will be surprised to hear that I think art is okay. I would much rather play soccer than draw, paint or do any other art activity. Art is my worst class. Every time I try drawing or sculpting, it ends up being ugly. I would be happy to never have to take another art class. But there are people in my class who like art, so we shouldn't cut out art for everyone just because people like myself don't like it. Maybe some day I will like going to art galleries to see the paintings and sculptures. I like the posters in my room, so I already like some art. Maybe I'll even buy a painting some day.

We saw some Inuit soapstone sculptures at the museum last week. The narwhales with their long tusks looked vicious. Seeing those sculptures made me think about life as an Inuit. It would be hard work. If I hadn't seen the sculptures, I wouldn't know about Inuit. That's another good reason for having arts. They help to learn about different people.

So even though I don't like doing art, I think that we should keep art. We'd miss art if we didn't have it.

Figure 4.6 Student's persuasive writing

Looking at Persuasive Writing

Title	Writer's position What is it? How did the writer communicate his/her position?	Support for this position What supporting information did the writer include? How and where did the writer include this information?	Arguments against this position What are the arguments? How did the writer present opposing arguments and how did she/he deal with those opposing ideas?

Figure 4.7 Looking at persuasive writing

Activity 4: Identifying features of non-narrative that instructs/directs

Our students have been instructing others about what they want and trying to direct others to get what they want from a very young age. Even before babies can talk, they use gestures, sounds, and facial expressions to direct their caregivers to feed them or bring them a toy, for example. As students go through school, their need to instruct or direct others does not diminish, although the topics for the instructions and directions become more complex.

In this activity, students compare and contrast two types of writing that instruct and direct. The poster in figure 4.8 explains a healthy lifestyle while figure 4.9 shows a "recipe" for healthy living. Students can use the chart in figure 4.10 to guide their analysis of the two non-narrative texts.

Students will likely note that instructive or directive texts tend to present information in steps or lists and tend to use specific verbs that have the implied "you" as their subject. Students might comment on what they have learned from the two texts and what further information they would like writers to include. They might also discuss the level of interest that the writers have generated in their writing and how they have made their writing interesting. When students write their own texts designed to instruct or direct, they can draw on their analysis of the two samples and of other writing found in their daily lives.

Do you want to stay HEALTHY and live a LONG LIFE?

It's not hard to figure out what to do.

- Eat fruits and vegetables every day

• Drink lots of water

- Eat small amounts of meat, carbohydrates, and dairy products

- Leave the junk food on the shelf at the store.

- Get enough sleep.

- Be active every day.

Figure 4.8 Poster explaining a healthy lifestyle

Recipe for Healthy Living

4-5 servings fruit and vegetables

2-3 servings carbohydrates

(bread, cereal, rice, pasta)

1-2 servings dairy products

(milk, cheese, yoghurt)

1-2 servings protein (meat, beans)

5-6 hours hard work

8-9 hours of sleep

6-8 glasses water

3-4 hours relaxation

1-2 hours physical activity

1-2 hours laughter

Eat the fruit, carbohydrates, dairy products, and meat three times each day. Drink the water throughout the day, though not too much before you go to bed, or you won't get the 8-9 uninterrupted hours of sleep. Plan for the physical activity and the relaxation each day. Work hard while you're at school so you learn lots. The laughter can happen any time (except in your sleep, of course!)

Figure 4.9 Recipe for healthy living

Thinking about Writing That Gives Instructions or Directions

Title	What do readers learn to do?	How are the ideas organized?	What kinds of words does the writer use to instruct or direct?

Figure 4.10 Thinking about writing that instructs or directs

Mini-Lessons: Content and Organization

Activity 1: Maintaining a focus

In this activity, students read a first draft (figure 4.11) and a final draft (figure 4.12) of one student's report on soil erosion. They will determine how well each draft stays on topic and what the writer did to tighten up the writing so the second draft was more focused. The following questions can be used to help students identify what writers can do to maintain the focus of their non-narrative texts.

1. Which title gives you more information about the topic of the essay?

2. What information do you get from the introductory paragraphs of each version? Which introductory paragraph stays on the same topic throughout the piece?

3. What are the key ideas of each paragraph in the two essays? Which paragraphs are easiest to follow – the ones with a single key idea or the one with many different ideas?

4. How does the writer connect each paragraph to the one before it? (What phrases or words does she/he use?)

5. After comparing and contrasting the two versions of the essay on soil erosion, what recommendations can you make to writers about staying on one topic?

First Draft

Soil Erosion

Soil erosion is a bad thing. Soil erosion can be prevented by planting trees to make wind breaks and by leaving grass strips between plots of land that have been ploughed. It gets really dusty when farmers plough all the fields every year. All that dust goes into other people's yards.

    Farm animals that eat the grass down to the dirt make it easier for soil to erode. These farm animals might be cows, sheep or horses. Farmers plow the soil and make the dirt powdery. Powdery dirt blows in the wind and gets in your eyes. No one likes dust and no one likes soil erosion.

Figure 4.11 First draft of report on soil erosion

Final Version

Soil Erosion and How to Avoid It

Don't take soil for granted. It will not always be under your feet if you allow wind and rain to let it erode. Whenever it rains, the raindrops move soil. Whenever it is windy, the wind picks up the soil and moves it.

People make soil erode faster by doing certain things. When farmers allow cows, sheep and horses to eat the grass down to the dirt, or when they plow the soil too much so it's like powder, they make soil erosion happen faster. People who cut down all the trees on a hill make the soil looser so it will erode faster. Once soil is gone, plants have nothing to grow in.

We don't have to let that happen. Soil erosion can be prevented by planting trees to make wind breaks and by leaving grass strips between plots of land that have been ploughed. Plants and trees prevent soil erosion. They slow down rain water so that it soaks into the ground rather than pushing the soil along. The roots also hold the soil down so it can't be washed away.

Think about soil erosion whenever you dig up plants or trees or whenever you dig in the dirt. If you let the wind and rain wash all the soil away, what will be left of your backyard?

Figure 4.12   Final version of report on soil erosion

Activity 2: Supporting the main point with examples and details

In this activity, students assess how well the writer has supported his main ideas with examples and details. They use the writers notes to determine what revisions he might make to provide stronger support for his position. In figure 4.13, the report compares and contrasts the lives of the Caboclos and the settlers living in the Amazon basin. You might use the following questions to focus students' attention on the writer's use of supporting details:

- What is the writer's main point?

- What details and examples provide information about the main point?

- What other information could the writer have included in the report?

- Where could the writer have included this information?

Students work with a partner or as a whole class to revise the report, adding the information from the writer's notes (see figure 4.14) and other information they find in books and magazines or on the Internet.

Life In the Amazon Basin with the Caboclos and the Settlers

Two groups of people live in the Amazon basin, the Caboclos and the settlers. The Caboclos are different from the settlers. They grow different crops and travel in different ways.

They are the same because they both try to grow things on the land and end up causing environmental damage. The soil is poor, so it's hard for them to grow things. Life isn't easy in the Amazon basin for Caboclos or settlers.

Figure 4.13 Report on Caboclos and settlers living in Amazon basin

Compare/Contrast Chart

Overall Topic: Notes taken from Waterlow, J. *The Amazon*. East Sussex, UK: Wayland, 1992.

Differences

Caboclos	Settlers
• European and Indian mixed race – have always lived there	• come from poorer areas with hope of creating a comfortable lifestyle for themselves
• live by the Amazon River – bananas are sold and transported by boat down the river	• settle beside roads because goods are transported by road
• catch fish and grow manioc and bananas	• raise cattle but pasture dies and weeds grow
• paddle on the river to go places	• clear land to grow cash crops like coffee
• live in thatched roof or corrugated metal roof homes	• population trebled between 1970 and 1980

Similarities

- live in Amazon basin
- crops can't be grown because of poor soil
- have to clear land frequently because soil is infertile
- long-lasting damage to the environment

Figure 4.14 Student's notes on Caboclos and settlers living in Amazon basin

Activity 3: Including quotes from references

For the most part, we want non-narrative writing to be in the students' own words. This is encouraged for the simple reason that word-for-word copying from any sources does not foster deep thinking about the topic. We explain plagiarism to students, and we caution against it over and over in our teaching. Sometimes, however, quotes are needed and can add to the student's writing. Explaining how and when to use quotes is often difficult, and students have some trouble deciding what is appropriate and what is not.

There are two main questions that need to be answered: (1) How much of the quote should be used, especially if the original text is very long? (2) How many quotes can be included so as not to overwhelm the student's own writing? These questions can be very difficult for students, even at the graduate level. When many long passages are included in a paper, it becomes difficult to figure out what our student writers are thinking. When quotes dominate a paper, there is no coherent flow of the student writer's thought. Frequent quotes scattered throughout a paper can chop up the writing and make it hard to follow. When used properly, quotes should support the writer and add to clarity to thoughts.

Figure 4.15 provides tips to help students decide when and how to use quotes. These suggestions are not hard and fast rules, but they help to avoid the problems that many students have in their writing. Figure 4.16 shows a good example of one student's use of quotes.

Using Quotes in Non-Narrative Writing

How many quotes should I use in my writing?

1. Summarize ideas or paraphrase what is written in print resources you use.

2. Explain your idea and then use a quote to help support that idea.

3. Make sure that any quote adds to what you want to say. Try to avoid using quotes just because they sound good.

4. Quotes are especially helpful when they come from someone who was an eyewitness to or took part in an event. If you are writing a biography, for example, use quotes from the person you are writing about to give readers a better sense of what the person was/is like.

How should I incorporate quotes into my writing?

1. Always use quotation marks "…" to enclose the words that are quoted.

2. In parenthesis, write the last name of the original writer, the year that the text was published, and the page number where you found the quote. For example: (Smith 2005, 10)

3. Always start a sentence with your own idea, and finish it with the quote.

4. You can start a sentence with the name of the original author followed by a verb such as "states," "explains," or "writes." Put the quote in quotation marks.

5. The sentences before and after the quote should relate to the quote. In fact, the sentence following the quote should explain parts of it or show how the quote fits in with your idea. It explains why you used the quote.

6. Try to use as few words from the original source as possible. A good guideline is to use no more than three sentences. This will vary. Remember, lengthy quotes break up the flow of the writing and sometimes steer the writing away from your own ideas.

Figure 4.15 Using quotes in non-narrative writing

One Student's Use of Quotes

How Coffee and Doughnuts Mix With Hockey: The Story of Tim Hortons

Tim Horton was a defenseman who started playing in the NHL in 1952 with the Toronto Maple Leafs. He was known as "the strongest man ever to lace up skates in the National Hockey League" (Hockey Hall of Fame and Museum, 2001-2003, unpaged). Montreal Canadien John Ferguson knew how tough Horton was. He said, "*Horton's the hardest bodychecker I've ever come up against. He's as strong as an ox and hits with terrific force*" (Shea, 2003, unpaged). The Leafs won four Stanley Cups while Horton played with them. In 1969, he was traded to the New York Rangers, then to the Pittsburgh Penguins, and finally to the Buffalo Sabres. In 1973, he was named the Sabres' Most Valuable Player at the age of 43.

Tim Horton realized that he could not gain financial security through his hockey income. He and his partner, Jim Charade, opened hamburger restaurants that were unsuccessful before they had the idea to sell coffee and doughnuts. Tim Horton continued to play hockey as more and more doughnut stores opened up.

On February 21, 1974, Tim Horton was killed in a car crash driving back to Buffalo after playing a game in Toronto. He was driving the sports car that the Sabres had given him as a bonus for signing that year.

Tim Horton was recognized for his hockey playing, as he entered the Hockey Hall of Fame in 1977. His name is known by hockey fans and doughnut eaters, as there are 2000 or more stores bearing his name. Jamie Fitzpatrick (2005, unpaged) says that because of his coffee shops, "Tim Horton ranks with Henderson, Howe, Orr, Hull, Richard and Number 99 as one of Canada's most famous hockey players."

References

Fitzpatrick, J. *Tim Horton: Hockey legend and fast food icon,* 2005.
   http://proicehockey.about.com/od/history/a/tim_horton.htm.
Hockey Hall of Fame and Museum (2001-2003). *Tim Horton.* www.legend-
   sofhockey.net:8080/LegendsOfHockey/jsp/LegendsMember.jsp?mem =
   p197702andtype = Playerandpage = bioandlist.
Shea, K. *One on One with Tim Horton,* 2003.
   www.legendsofhockey.net/html/spot_oneononep197702.htm

Figure 4.16 A paper using quotes

Activity 4: Audience awareness: Using elements of graphic design

We all know that the layout of a page, the style of font, and the manner in which material is presented are important to our interest in and understanding of the material. As a writer, awareness of audience perceptions and motivations is key to communicating important messages. Regardless of whether writers use computers or their own penmanship to write, they should consider the arrangement of the text and graphics on their page. Students of any age are more conscious than ever of the role graphic design plays in their lives. These students often include elements of design in their written assignments automatically, without being told to do so. This activity adds to their repertoire.

Graphic design includes both page layout and typography (Moline 1995). The page layout is the positioning of print and all the other visual elements of the work. Laying out a page means paying attention to the arrangement of text into paragraphs or columns, and the use of headings, borders, arrows, lines, bullets, and so on. Layout helps writers organize information, make connections between text and graphics, and highlight certain important information. Typography, or type style, includes not only the font, but also the size of font and its style, whether bold, italicized, or underlined. Figure 4.17 identifies some layout and typography features that students might consider when designing the final drafts of their content-area writing.

Graphic Design: Things You Can Do

Lines and White Space

- Separate graphics and text by drawing a line across or down a page.
- Highlight and separate text or graphics by drawing boxes around them.
- Give readers' eyes a break by leaving lots of white space around the text and graphics.

Font

- Emphasize words, titles, headings, or phrases using:

  bold type   ALL CAPS   *italics*

  <u>underlining</u>   larger font size

- Convey the tone or mood of your writing through the font:

  Times New Roman   a formal typeface used in books and newspapers

  Andy   a less formal typeface that looks like carefree printing

  AvantGarde   a bold font that works well for headings

  Arial   a fairly formal font that is easy to read

Heading and Subheadings
Usually, headings work in levels:

**The First Level Is Usually the Title of Your Writing.
It Stands Out by Being Centred and is often ALL CAPS or
In Larger Font Size. It May Be Bold or <u>Underlined</u>.**

Second-Level Headings Stand Apart from the Paragraphs that Follow Them,
Usually by Being in Title Case and/or by Being Centred. They may be underlined.

<u>Third-level headings also stand apart from the paragraphs that follow them. Usually they are flush with the left margin. They may be underlined.</u>

Figure 4.17 Graphic design: Things you can do

REFERENCES

Booth, D. *Even Hockey Players Read: Boys, Literacy and Learning.* Markham, ON: Pembroke, 2002.

Clay, M. *What Did I Write?* Portsmouth, NH: Heinemann, 1975.

Halliday, M. A. K. *Learning How to Mean.* New York, NY: Elsevier North-Holland, Inc., 1975.

Harvey, S. "Nonfiction Inquiry: Using Real Reading and Writing to Explore the World." *Language Arts, 80(1)*, 12-22, 2002.

Hidi, S. and A. Hildyard. "The Comparison of Oral and Written Productions in Two Discourse Types." *Discourse Process, 6*, 91-105, 1983.

Kamberelis, G. "Genre Development and Learning: Children Writing Stories, Science Reports," and Poems. *Research in the Teaching of English, 33,* 403-460, 1999.

Moline, S. *I See What You Mean: Children at Work with Visual Information.* Markham, ON: Pembroke, 1995.

Sowers, S. "The Story and the "All About" Book". In J. Hansen, T. Newkirk, D. Graves (Eds.). *Breaking Ground: Teachers Relate Reading and Writing in the Elementary School.* Portsmouth, NH: Heinemann, 1985.

CHAPTER 5

WRITING POETRY ACROSS THE CURRICULUM

Poems hang out where life is.

(Susan Goldsmith Wooldridge 1996, p.4)

WHY WRITE POETRY IN CONTENT AREAS?

Imagine that poetry does not leap to mind when considering writing possibilities within content areas. Yet, Wooldridge (above) places poetry squarely in the middle of everyday life, which is where most topics in science, social studies, music, art, mathematics, and health are also found. Poetry has untapped potential for communicating and discovering in all subject areas, because it is hidden in so many of the things we encounter in everyday life. Corrigan (2002) says that students "need to see the concrete, work-a-day manner in which poetry is and can be woven into their existence" (p.33). Content-area classes provide many opportunities for concrete, hands-on experiences. In this chapter, I provide suggestions for using poetry to capture the learning that comes from these experiences.

Poetry provides a vibrant forum for thinking, as it allows students to distill experience using a few words. Booth and Moore (2003) say, "the more we mess about with words, the more intrigued with words do we become. The more words we have at our disposal, the better we can think, thus the better we can write" (p.106). At the same time that students are playing with words to create a poem, they are also playing with ideas. That is a great place for learning to happen. When writing poetry, students are like scientists. They become attentive to the sensory information in their world and to the clues in the texts they read (Cullinan, Scala, and Schroder 1995). As they trim away extraneous words and replace vague words with more precise ones, students refine and sharpen their understanding of the ideas.

Some teachers keep poetry writing on the margins because it seems so difficult and inaccessible. These apprehensions are fairly widespread. I recently read about a study that Strenski and Esposito conducted back in 1980. When they asked their college students to define poetry, the students focused on the importance of rhythm, rhyme, and punctuation. They judged the merit of a poem on how difficult it was to understand. This study was conducted decades ago, but I wonder if we would find similar results if the study were carried out in today's grades 4-8 classrooms. All too often, I have observed students writing couplets or quatrains that make little sense, but have impeccable rhyme schemes. These students devote so much energy to finding rhyming words that they lose track of what they want to say in their poems. Keeping track of the number of syllables and finding rhyming words may distract students from communicating their intended message.

Yet, poetry does not have to be difficult if we encourage students to focus on meaning and playing with words. When students write list poems and free verse, for example, they do not have to get caught up in the demands of rhyme and rhythm schemes. Robert Frost (in Robertson 1997, p.167) says that "writing free verse is like playing tennis with the net down." Just as it takes much less effort for tennis players to hit a ball onto the opponent's court when the net is down, it is easier for our students to say something worthwhile when writing poetry that is not constrained by rules for rhyme and meter.

In this chapter, you will find ideas for encouraging students to pay attention to words and ideas. The chapter begins with a list of suggested avenues for inviting poetry writing in various content-area subjects. It then moves to teaching ideas for developing students' abilities to craft poems as they deepen their content-area learning.

IDEAS FOR WRITING POETRY ACROSS THE CURRICULUM

Social Studies

- Poem for two voices comparing the distinguishing features of early civilizations

- Cinquain about historical figures who have contributed to the development of the country and the world (e.g., political figures, inventors)

Science

- Riddle about sounds of everyday life and how they are produced

- Chant about energy conservation

Mathematics

- Rhyming couplet to help memorize multiplication basic facts

- Question/answer poem consisting of probability problems and their answers. For example:

  How many times does a red
  End up in my hand
  When I tip the M and M bag?
  One in seven, my friend,
  Try it yourself.
  It's one in seven.

Art

- Free-verse poem describing a favourite painting or sculpture

- Rhyming couplet used as a title for a painting or sculpture the student has created

Health

- Haiku about healthy relationships with friends, family, and peers

- Shape poem about healthy and not-so-healthy food choices

Music

- Rewrite the lyrics to well-known folk songs

- Clap four or five bars in 2/4, 3/4, or 4/4 time. Students string words together, matching the rhythm you clap, to create a chant.

HELPING STUDENTS BECOME BETTER POETRY WRITERS

According to Georgia Heard (1990, p.65) there are two types of tools that writers can use to craft poetry:

1. meaning tools (e.g., image, metaphor, line breaks, and titles)

2. music tools (e.g., rhyme, repetition/patterns, rhythm, and alliteration)

These tools are like the lines, colours, and shapes that visual artists use to create paintings. Just as artists try out thick, thin, wavy, or straight lines to see what effect they will have on the overall composition of the painting, poets play with various ways to break up phrases to determine how the flow and the meaning of their poetry will be affected. Helping students use these tools may involve identifying examples in published poetry, but that is only a small part of teaching the craft of poetry writing. From there, we provide ample space for students to use these tools as they write poems that delight readers.

Two creative skills should be added to this list of things that poets identify as essential to their writing:

1. colection of procise words

2. trimming phrases down to their essence

Patrick Lane says, "poets still pay attention to each word, you see." He goes even further, declaring that "most prose is sloppy, flabby poetry at best" (in Bowling 2002, p.70). Lane's assertion may seem extreme, but he certainly makes the point that poets are very selective in their word choices. Michael Ondaatje explains that he revises and shapes his poems in an effort to "remove all those extra clothes that were there" in the early drafts of a poem (in Bowling 2002, p.34). A clear picture of poetry writing emerges from these two poets' descriptions – the craft of writing poetry involves ensuring that the writing is lean and not overdressed with unnecessary words!

All of this attention to word meanings is very likely to translate into deeper learning of concepts you are teaching in your content classes. The teaching suggestions that follow help students think about the words and ideas that arise from content-area units as they write poetry.

Mini-Lessons: Meaning and Music Tools

Activity 1: Experimenting with line breaks

Georgia Heard (1999, p.84) says that poets work with the "tension between sound and silence," thinking about the words and the "silence between the words." The poem's rhythm is created not only in the accents and syllables of the words, but also in the lines and where they are broken on the page. Line breaks can occur where readers would naturally take a breath or where poets want to emphasize certain words. Poets might change the pace of a poem or create tension by using a technique called *enjambment*, where the natural rhythm or meaning of a line is interrupted by being carried onto the next line.

In this activity, students play with sentences from a content-area textbook or trade book, or from their own writing, to get a sense of how the meaning and rhythm change depending on where the lines are broken.

To support students in developing a sense of how they can use line breaks in their poetry writing, I suggest copying the sentences in figure 5.1 onto an overhead transparency. You and your students can experiment with where the line breaks are placed. It is helpful to have students read aloud the results of the group efforts to see how the line breaks influence the way they read and the way they think about the ideas in the sentence. Students can trade their poems with a partner to compare and contrast what they have done and how the rhythms and meanings are different as a result of the different line breaks. In the two examples of where line breaks might occur in the sentence, therefore, the nouns that are alone on one line are emphasized (see figure 5.2). We get a sense that the writer wants us to consider them very carefully.

Students can then either take additional sentences from a content-area book to play with line breaks independently or write their own poems about an activity, experiment, field trip, interview, or observation to practice playing with line breaks.

Experiment with line breaks as you create a poem from this sentence:

Mountains can make the weather wetter – or drier – than nearby areas. When warm, moist winds sweep up the side of a mountain, clouds form and rain falls. On the other side of the mountain it may be desert-like.
(Wyatt and Share 2000, p.7).

Figure 5.1 Sentences that can be used for making line breaks

How do the two poems below give you a different impression of the effect of mountains on weather? Which words are emphasized in each one? What do you do differently when you read each poem aloud? What makes you read them differently?

Mountains can make the weather wetter –
or drier –
than nearby areas.
When warm, moist winds
sweep up the side of a mountain,
clouds form
and rain falls. On the other side
of the mountain
it may be desert-like.

Mountains
can make the weather wetter – or drier –
than nearby areas.
When warm, moist winds
sweep
up the side of a mountain,
clouds form
and rain falls.
On the other side of the mountain
it may be
desert-like.

Figure 5.2 Examples of line-break use

Activity 2: Using repetition of words, sounds, or lines

David Booth and Bill Moore (2003) write that poems "make our ears sing" (p.26). The music is created by the sounds of individual words (e.g., using onomatopoeia – words that sound like the things they describe). Music is also found in the sounds of words placed together (e.g., rhymes – parts of words sound the same; alliteration – words in a phrase start with the same sound; consonance – words in a phrase or sentence have similar consonant sounds in the middle or at the end of the words; or assonance – words in a phrase or sentence have similar vowel sounds, but they may not rhyme). Sometimes repeating words or phrases brings out the musicality of poems, as well.

In this activity, you draw students' attention to the sounds of the language in poems and invite them to use repeated sounds, words, or phrases to make their poems sing. As with the line break activity, students play around with the possibilities for using poets' tools, in this case the tool of repetition.

The activity could start with a paragraph from a content-area textbook or trade book on a topic. It could also start with notes from reading a textbook, or from an activity, field trip, interview, or observation. In the example in figure 5.3a, the seventh-grade boy, Ashif, used notes taken from a presentation and a website that can be used later to create a poem (figure 5.3b).

To support students' use of the tool of repetition, you might make copies of a paragraph from a text you are using, double-spacing it to give students room to write. Invite students to underline words that are really important. Then ask them to think of words that rhyme with the underlined words that start with the same letter, or that have the same vowel or consonant sounds in the middle or at the end of the words. It is often helpful to use a dictionary to generate the words. Students also play around with words and phrases that they could repeat for emphasis. Students keep these words in mind as they compose their poems, but their focus is on saying something about the topic. They might use one or two of the words from their list, or they might use many words. The goal is to play with repeated sounds and words but not to lose the sense of the poem for the sake of repeating sounds.

Ashif's Notes From a Website and Presentation From Health Nurse

Topic: Harmful effects of smoking

Sources: www.cancer.org/docroot/PED/ped_10_1.asp?sitearea = PED
Health Nurse presentation

Notes	Thoughts
• Each year, nearly 1 of every 5 deaths in USA related to smoking. About 87% of lung cancer deaths caused by smoking. Smoking causes heart disease, lung, larynx, oral, esophagus, bladder, and pancreas cancer.	• If everyone quit smoking, there would be a lot more people still alive.
• Tobacco products contain nicotine. Nicotine is addictive and poisonous. More than 60 compounds that cause cancer are found in cigarettes — include ammonia, tar, and carbon monoxide.	• Why would anyone want to take something that is poisonous?
• Carbon monoxide is emitted (400 times greater than what is considered safe in industrial settings). Carbon monoxide interferes with ability of blood to transport oxygen to body.	• So that's why people who smoke have a hard time running and climbing stairs and stuff.
• In 1988, the US Surgeon General said that being addicted to nicotine is like being addicted to drugs such as heroin and cocaine.	• My uncle has been smoking for 35 years. He says he can't quit. He's addicted.

Repeated sounds:

nicotine	addictive	smoking	heart disease
needles	admire	sorry	heart-stopping
magazine	active	swimming	please
been	address	smile	harm

tobacco	oxygen	carbon monoxide	cancer
tempo	odd	cartoon	sir
toast	again	messes	candy
whacko	auditorium	carry	candle

In his poem, Ashif used a few of the words from his list. He liked the sound of the word, nicotine and decided to repeat it.

Figure 5.3a Ashif uses notes and the tool of repetition to create a poem on health

---

Smoke and You'll be Sorry!

Tobacco has nicotine, nicotine,
Don't know it's addictive –
Where have you been?

Smoking is harmful.
You'll get heart disease and cancer.
Yes sir,
The carbon monoxide messes up
Blood carrying oxygen.
Don't make me say it again.

Tobacco has nicotine, nicotine.
And it is addictive –
You know what I mean!

Figure 5.3b Ashif uses the tool of repetition to write a poem

Activity 3: Creating images of concrete experiences

Poets try to help readers "imagine, visualize, and, ultimately, bring [readers] closer to the experience of the poem" (Booth and Moore 2003, p.64). In this activity, students attempt to do just that by creating visual images and helping readers imagine the sounds, smells, and textures of the experiences communicated in their poetry. The activity works well in response to hands-on activities.

I use a published poem to illustrate what students can do in their own writing. Florence McNeil (in Booth 1989, p.48) has written a poem about a trip to a park to observe bugs. The poem is in figure 5.4 for you to reproduce as an overhead transparency.

Water Bugs in My Notebook

I went to a pond with my class
to put water bugs in my notebook
My teacher said
write everything you see
in the pond.

And so I did.

I saw a water strider
with long legs
like pole vaults with hinges
walking on top of the water.

It left a dimple in the water
Where it stepped.

I saw a round black
backswimmer

moving away from its head
with quick, short back strokes.

The water strider didn't pay attention
To the backswimmer
And the backswimmer ignored
The water strider.

I was the only one
Paying attention to both of them.

Figure 5.4 Poem creating images from real-life experiences

After reading the poem aloud to enjoy the sounds and rhythms, students focus on the pictures the words have created in their minds. They can draw or paint the pictures, or talk about them with a partner. Students then focus on the words and phrases that this poet used to create her images, noting the simile.

Following the discussion, students write their own poems. They might begin by writing words and phrases that capture a concrete experience they have had in class or on a field trip, or they can plunge right into writing their poems. The phrases might simply be tools for remembering the experience, or they might end up in the poems that students write.

Ratiba, a grade-six student, wrote about her experience working with pastels in art class (see figure 5.5).

Smudgey Fun in Art Class

Crayons slide on paper
like skates on ice.

Not a cloud in the sky blue
is my favourite colour. I used it
a lot
to draw kites.

My hand rubbed on the kites
accidentally
and they had
blue tails in funny places.
Blue smudges
on the pink flowers and the kids flying the kites.

Today I used pastels in art.

Figure 5.5 Ratiba's poem creating images of art experience

Activity 4: Writing titles

Titles usually give readers a sense of what the poem is about, but they can also provide just enough information to create suspense or raise questions about the topic. Often, titles are the first lines of a poem.

In this activity, students' attention is drawn to possibilities for titles, as they read through and identify how titles of published poetry contribute to the poems. In preparation, gather published poetry for students to read, drawing from the list at the end of this chapter (p.83) or your own collection. With a partner, students read five or six poems, recording the title and what the title contributes to the poem. For example, the title of the water bug poem in figure 5.4 summarizes what the poem is about. Students are likely to find that many poems use the first line as the title. There will be variations, however. Some poems use the title as part of the first line. David McCord's "I Have a Book" is one example (in Cullinan 1996, 7). Here is how it starts:

I Have a Book
that has no cover
where there used to be a lady
and her knighted lover.

Students can compare with other groups what they have found out about the contributions titles make to poetry. As a class, draw conclusions about titles for poems.

Students then create two or three possible titles for their own poems. I recommend that titles be created after the poems are written because writers often are not entirely clear on what their poems will be about until they have written them. This adds to the discovery through writing.

Mini-Lessons: Staying Lean and Removing the Extra Layers

Activity 1: Creating a list poem on overhead transparency strips

In this activity, students create a class poem by writing short phrases on strips of overhead transparencies. The teacher works with students to arrange the plastic strips into a smooth-flowing poem that communicates what they have learned about a content-area topic. It is the best activity I know for fostering a frugal, discerning attitude toward choosing words. Because students write on small strips of acetate with wide-point overhead transparency pens, they have no choice but to write a few well-chosen, meaning-laden words. For this reason, the activity is particularly effective for developing note-taking skills. I have seen this activity used with great success in every subject area from grades 4-8.

To prepare for the activity, cut up overhead transparencies into strips that are approximately 2.5cm by 1cm. Divide the class into groups of three students. Distribute several of these strips and overhead pens to each group. Have copies of materials that students can read to gather information about the content-area topic. I generally ask younger students to read 1-2 paragraphs from trade books or textbooks on the topic and older students to read 1-2 pages. In the example from a fifth-grade class, I gave students 5-6 pages of advertisements from teen magazines (see figure 5.6). Students could also gather information from watching videos, completing hands-on activities, or participating in field trips.

Using as few words as possible, students write one idea from their reading, video, activity, or field trip on each overhead strip. They often use a noun and verb with a few other essential words. They bring their strips (I usually encourage one or two per student) to the overhead projector. You and your students can reorganize and combine phrases to create a poem that you are all happy with. You may decide as a group to create a phrase that can be repeated as a refrain, as well. Students can then create their own poems independently or with a partner.

Students write *list poems* about differences between "real life" girls or boys and those portrayed in the media to gain a better understanding of how the media influences body image.

Two fifth-grade girls wrote these poems:

Magazine Ad Girls	**Real Life Girls**
Don't each much,	Sometimes eat too much,
Are very skinny,	Sometimes go on diets,
Wear designer clothes,	Can be all sorts of sizes,
Have cute faces,	Are cute in their own way,
Don't have zits,	Pop zits every other day,
Have perfect figures.	Come in many shapes.

Figure 5.6 List poems

Activity 2: Two-voice poems: Compare and contrast information

This type of poem works well when you want students to compare and contrast information on two topics. It is modelled after Paul Fleischman's (1988) *Joyful Noise: Poems for Two Voices*. To gather and organize information for the poems, students should complete a compare/contrast chart such as the one in chapter 3, p.36.

The example in figure 5.7 can be used to demonstrate how students might create a poem for two voices from notes organized in the compare/contrast chart. Two eighth-grade students wrote the poem for their social studies unit on

Canadian history. Students can note how the two voices sometimes speak together, as indicated by having the phrase in the middle of the page. When the voices speak together, they talk of things they have in common. When readers read the separate parts, they are speaking of differences between the two men.

When I use this example, I point out how the writers combined some information from their notes on the compare/contrast form (see page 37) and decided not to use some of the other information. I point out how the boys used key words from their compare/contrast chart and didn't rewrite everything from the chart in their poem. My students and I then write a poem together as a class using compare/contrast chart notes for a topic we are studying. Students follow up by writing their own compare/contrast poems.

Two eighth-grade boys wrote the following poem for two voices to communicate what they had learned from reading about key people who contributed to confederation in Canada.

We Helped to Bring Confederation to Canada

Voice of Sir George-Étienne Cartier	**Voice of Sir John A. Macdonald**
I am French Canadian.	I am a Scottish immigrant.
I supported the Lower Canada	I supported business, railways
rebellion and fled to the USA.	and the Anglican Church.

We were elected to the legislature.

I'm Canada East.	I'm Canada West.

Heard of the Great Coalition? That was us (and George Brown).

New federation? It's great for better	New federation? I wrote 72 Resolutions
understanding between French	
and English	

Charlottetown, Quebec, London. We were there 1864 to 1866.
Confederation Rocks!

Figure 5.7 Poem for two voices

Activity 3: Distilling poems from paragraphs

In addition to helping students develop their poetry-writing skills, this is an excellent activity for developing note-taking skills. Start by making an overhead transparency of a paragraph from a content book. I recommend that you think aloud, demonstrating to students how to select the words that are essential to communicating the gist of the paragraph. Shape those words into a poem. In figure 5.8 you will find an example that is appropriate for grade-six students.

The homes of animals are always changing. Some changes happen in nature, and others are caused by people. When an animal's habitat, or living area, is no longer the same, that animal must adapt, or change, to suit its new habitat. (Kalman, 2000, p.4).

Why Do Animals Adapt?
Animal homes
(or habitats)
Are always changing.
Sometimes nature is the cause,
Sometimes people are.
Animals change
To suit their new habitat.

Figure 5.8 Distilling a poem from a paragraph

Activity 4: Writing from content-area vocabulary lists

Our refrigerator, like those of many friends, has a scatter of words on magnets that we put together to create silly/provocative/profound messages. This activity works just like the refrigerator magnet words. Students create poems from a collection of words that are important in the topic of study. As they write their poems, they will be thinking about the concepts and applying what they have learned. The activity is great for building vocabulary, as well as for developing students' poetry writing repertoires.

I suggest that you introduce the activity by composing a poem together with your students. The poem will be based on vocabulary from the unit of study. I find it helpful to include nouns, verbs, and adjectives in the list. I include the words that are important in the unit of study and words that I particularly like, called "wild words." These words are taken from other poems, songs, or stories and can be used in the same way as wild cards in a card game. In figure 5.9, there are lists of nouns, verbs, adjectives, and "wild words" pulled from other poetry books.

As a group, decide how many words from the list should be included in the poem. As shown in figure 5.9, in a poem created by grade-four students, you can add words and modify the form, if needed (e.g., change verbs to nouns).

List of words for geometry unit:

square	slurp	construct	congruent	frying pan
trapezoid	hockey	translate	symmetrical	pizza
line	elbow	rotate	parallel	marshmallow
rectangle	burn	draw	three-dimensional	howling

Poem we created:

Hockey Rinks are Rectangles for a Reason
We tried to construct
a trapezoid hockey rink
yesterday.
Scoring goals is harder –
The sides are not congruent.
You go deeper in the corner
On one side
With the defense's elbows
Holding you back.

Where do we draw the blue line?
How do we set up the goals
across from each other?
Only two sides are parallel.

Trapezoid hockey rinks
Get hockey players howling
Hockey rinks are rectangles for a reason.

Figure 5.9 Poem created from a list of geometry words

REFERENCES

Booth, D., and B. Moore. *Poems Please: Sharing Poetry with Children.* 2nd Ed. Toronto, ON: Pembroke, 2003.

Bowling, T. *Where the Words Come From: Canadian Poets in Conversation.* Roberts Creek, BC: Nightwood Editions, 2002.

Corrigan, P. "Handing Down Knowledge: A Poetic Apprenticeship." *Voices from the Middle, 10*(2), 33-37, 2002.

Cullinan, B. E., M. C. Scala, and V. C. Schroder. *Three Voices: An Invitation to Poetry Across the Curriculum.* Toronto, ON: Pembroke, 1995.

Frost, R. Quoted in Robertson, C. (Ed.). *The Dictionary of Quotations.* Hertfordshire, UK: Wordsworth Editions Ltd., 1997.

Heard, G. *Awakening the Heart: Exploring Poetry in Elementary and Middle School.* Portsmouth, NH: Heinemann, 1990.

Strenski, E., and N. G. Esposito. "The Poet, the Computer, and the Classroom." *College English, 42*, 142-150, 1980.

Nonfiction

Kalman, B. *How Do Animals Adapt?* St. Catharines, ON: Crabtree Publishing, 2000.

Wyatt, V., and B. Share. *Weather.* Toronto, ON: Kids Can Press, 2000.

Poetry Collections

Booth, D. (Compiled by) *Til All the Stars Have Fallen: Canadian Poems for Children.* Toronto, ON: Kids Can Press, 1989.

Cullinan, B. (Ed.). *A Jar of Tiny Stars: Poems by NCTE Award-Winning Poets.* Honesdale, PA: Boyds Mills Press, 1996.

Eliot, T. S. *Old Possum's Book of Practical Cats.* London, UK: Faber and Faber, 1939.

Esbensen, B. *Echoes for the Eye: Poems to Celebrate Patterns in Nature.* New York, NY: HarperCollins, 1996.

Fitch, S. *If You Could Wear My Sneakers!* Toronto, ON: Doubleday, 1997.

Fleischman, P. *Joyful Noise: Poems for Two Voices.* New York, NY: Harper Trophy, 1988.

Hopkins, L. B. *Spectacular Science: A Book of Poems.* New York, NY: Simon and Shuster Books for Young Readers, 1999.

Hughes, T. *Scary Poems for Rotten Kids.* Windsor, ON: Black Moss Press, 1982.

Korman, G., and B. Korman. *The Last-place Sports Poems of Jeremy Bloom: A Collection of Poems About Winning, Losing, and Being a Good Sport (Sometimes).* New York, NY: Scholastic, 1996.

Lee, D. *Garbage Delight: Another Helping.* Toronto, ON: Key Porter Kids, 2002.

Lesynski, L. *Nothing Beats a Pizza.* Toronto, ON: Annick Press, 2001.

Little, J. *Hey World, Here I Am!* Toronto, ON: Kids Can Press, 1986.

Rosen, M. *No Breathing in Class.* London, UK: Puffin Books, 2002.

Worth, V. *Small Poems Again.* New York, NY: Farrar, Strauss and Giroux, 1986.

CHAPTER 6

WRITING NARRATIVE ACROSS THE CURRICULUM

> The drive to story is basic in all human beings. Stories shape
> our lives and our culture – we cannot live without them.
> **(Bob Barton and David Booth 1990, p.12)**

WHY WRITE NARRATIVE IN CONTENT AREAS?

David Booth and Bob Barton make it clear that stories are essential to being human. We all have a basic need to organize and make sense of our experiences through narrative. Stories help us give structure "to our mountain of memories and emotions, making sense and giving cohesion to our lives" (Booth and Barton, 2002, p.8). When we read and write stories, we come to know ourselves and discover what contributions we might make to our world. The stories we write and read help us understand what is and envision what might be. Daily, we use stories to build relationships with others, finding that the stories of others entertain us and open our perspectives on the world. Through the ages, humans have used stories to teach and shape other's behaviour.

Today, our students encounter stories of their peers, family members, and community members while getting ready for school, while riding the bus, walking to school, or through the school hallways. They do not just hear the stories of people they know. Even if they do not read fiction, our students have stories available to them from every corner of the world every day. Newspapers, magazines, television, radio, and Internet information sources use narrative to convey social, scientific, or political information. Often, these stories follow individuals whose lives are affected by the major news events of each week. These local stories give meaning to the seemingly abstract events that are far removed from the experiences of many of our students.

We cannot deny that stories are part of students' worlds beyond the school curriculum. Why, then, would we not be able to find space for narrative within the content-area curricula? Social studies, health, science, art, mathematics, and music are all about the people, ideas, events, and the natural and human-created world. Gordon Wells (1984, p.194) tells us that there is plenty of room for narrative. He explains that storying, is:

> ...an activity that pervades all aspects of learning... stories are one of the most effective ways of making one's own interpretation of events and ideas available to others. Through the exchange of stories, therefore, teachers and students can share their understandings of a topic . . . In this sense, stories and storying are relevant in all areas of the curriculum."

We add a personal dimension to curriculum content by inviting students to write stories about their learning. Students use narrative structures to breathe life into the concepts and ideas that curriculum documents identify as key learning objectives. Content knowledge becomes more relevant and understandable when connected to the experiences of story characters. In addition, familiar and beloved narrative structures (e.g., introduction, initiating event leading to conflict that gets more intense until the protagonist solves the problem) provide dependable frameworks for pulling the content-area knowledge together into a cohesive whole. I found this to be the case with students writing in grade-six and grade-eight science classes. Most students wrote narratives when given the choice to use any genre to show what they had learned about simple machines. They told me that they found narrative writing easier and more enjoyable than poetry or non-narrative forms (for a short list of narrative forms see figure 6.0, on page 88.)

In spite of students' familiarity with the narrative genre, there are still challenges in writing narrative across the curriculum. In this chapter, three activities address students' need for assistance in weaving content knowledge into their stories. In addition, you will find ideas for encouraging students in writing narrative across the curriculum and mini-lessons for helping students develop character, plot, and style as they write engaging stories and extend their content-area knowledge.

IDEAS FOR WRITING NARRATIVE ACROSS THE CURRICULUM

Social Studies

- Write a series of diary entries telling a story of the everyday life of a particular group of people who are identified in the curriculum.

- Write a time slip fantasy as a character from today's world goes back in time to a setting from the social studies curriculum.

Science

- Write an adventure story showing how characters use simple machines to survive.

- Write an autobiography of a stream.

Mathematics

- Write a mystery where the detective must use what students learned in a measurement unit to solve the crime.

- Write a script for a radio play telling the story of a character who gains or loses large amounts of something. Students demonstrate what they have learned about adding and subtracting four-digit numbers in their story.

Art

- Write a story about a character who walks into a painting of the student's choice. How do the colours, the lines (e.g., smooth, flowing, horizontal, sharp, jagged, vertical), and the textures contribute to the way the character acts, talks, and feels when she/he gets inside?

- Write a science fiction/fantasy/realistic fiction/historical fiction story about a painter, showing what you know about primary, secondary, and tertiary colours.

Health

- Write a short play about characters who apply what students have learned about dealing with peer pressure related to substance use and abuse.

- Write a humourous or serious story (it could take the form of a cartoon) about a babysitting event showing what students have learned about caring for young children.

Music

- Write a biography of a musical instrument, describing its history, construction, and use (e.g., historical or period instrument such as the sackbut, or the instruments the students play in class).

- Write new words to familiar melodies, using students' knowledge of rhythm to ensure that the new text fits with the melody. The new words should tell a story.

NARRATIVE FORMS: A SHORT LIST

realistic fiction	cartoons	historical fiction
mystery	science fiction	fantasy
ballad	biography	diary
script for a play, film, radio show	script for a puppet show	folk tale
myth	legend	fable

Figure 6.0 Narrative forms: A short list

HELPING STUDENTS BECOME BETTER NARRATIVE WRITERS AND LEARN CONTENT KNOWLEDGE

Students have an authentic purpose for finding out as much as they can about a topic when they write stories in content areas. If they are writing about characters in a particular historical period, for example, they need information about the homes, food, entertainment, clothing, and family structures of the time. This next section presents activities for helping students use that information in their stories.

Mini-Lessons: Weaving Content Knowledge into Stories

Communicating content knowledge through narrative is one of the more difficult writing tasks our students can take up. They have read and listened to enough stories to know that readers do not appreciate wading through a pedantic litany of facts. Their sights are set on the characters and their actions. Yet, if our students focus only on the story, they might not be deepening their learning of the content-area concepts and perspectives. In my experience with students writing narrative in science, they are more likely to sacrifice content information than allow the story to be weighted down with detail. They have a strong sense of how stories work and want to entertain their audience. I applaud these intentions and generally do not want to discourage them when planning learning activities to help students weave content information into their narratives. When writing in content areas, however, an equally important goal is for students to learn the content-area concepts. Some students need support managing story and content demands.

Activity 1: Adapting familiar story lines and giving examples

In this activity, students assess one grade-eight student's narrative (see figure 6.1). It can be used as an example of possibilities or of things to avoid when writing their own narratives. It follows from an assignment where the student was to demonstrate what he knew about mechanical advantage, pulleys, levers, and gears in the writing genre of his choice. He made the task more manageable, as well as humorous and entertaining by adapting a familiar story, Charles Dickens' *A Christmas Carol*. Having a tale upon which to base his own story, he could concentrate on creating new twists that incorporated the science information. Craig included the terminology from his science classes, but has not given specific examples to demonstrate clearly what each term means.

These questions provide helpful starting points for discussing the story:

1. Where do you see evidence in this story that the writer included information from his science class?

2. What four science concepts does the story talk about? What do you learn about the four concepts?

3. What questions are unanswered? What could the writer have done to give readers a better understanding of what the science terms mean?

3. Summarize the plot of the story. Is it familiar to you?

4. What did Craig do to make it easier to write a story about the four science concepts?

5. What did Craig do to make the story entertaining? What else could he have done?

Following the discussion, students could look at the notes they have taken of the content concepts they are to demonstrate in a narrative. They can think about how they might adapt a familiar story line to suit their content-area purposes. Of course, they can also create their own plots. In any case, students should strive to give examples of the concepts, rather than just use the content vocabulary, in their stories.

Mechanical Advantage Haunts You

Jim was a very lazy and ignorant kid. "Who needs mechanical advantage!" he would always say. Of course, this always made his life harder, especially since he wasn't that strong himself. Soon he began to forget what mechanical advantage really was, and was simply lost in a world of hard work. He couldn't keep up with it, and his laziness only made matters worse. It seemed that there was no hope left for this poor soul. Fortunately for him, though, he was being watched. And hope would come sooner than he thought. One night he fell asleep, but right after he fell asleep, he found himself sitting on his bed.

"Ah, this is one odd dream," he said to himself. He turned around to see him or what seemed to be his "body" sleeping on his bed.

"OK, this is getting weird," he said. It would soon get weirder, for a shadowy figure emerged out of nowhere. Jim couldn't help letting out a high, girlish cry for help.

"SILENCE!" said the figure.

"I, the Ghost of Pulleys has appeared before you today to teach you a lesson. I am one of the three Ghosts of Mechanical Advantage. You have been very foolish lately, being ignorant about the power of mechanical advantage! Prepare to be educated!" Jim was quickly sucked into what seemed to be . . . a science classroom? There, standing in front of him was the Ghost of Pulleys.

"Now, it is time for your enlightenment. The pulley can greatly help you be reducing the force needed to lift an object, "Jim slowly, but surely began to understand how helpful pulleys were. Moveable pulleys, fixed pulleys, double pulleys, the works.

"So, the more sections of rope I have, the easier it is to lift?" Jim asked.

"Of course," replied the ghost.

After an adequate lesson with the Ghost of Pulleys, Jim was sent to the next ghost. A swirling vortex opened up before him and he jumped in.

Whoosh! Jim landed in a playground where he saw a see-saw in the middle, and a bunch of other things lying around, such as a hockey stick, a pair of shears, a hammer, and a crowbar.

"Alas, the uneducated mortal has arrived," sounded a booming voice.

"Let me guess," Jim replied, "The Ghost of Levers."

The ghost was very pleased, "Ah, that gets a lot of things out of the way. Now, it is time for your enlightenment." Jim was told about Class 1, Class 2 and Class 3 levers, as well as how you can find them in real life.

"Yes, levers can help you greatly when used correctly. Now for your final destination." The vortex appeared before Jim again and he jumped in, wondering what was next.

Tick-Tock, Tick-Tock, Tick-Tock.

"Where am I??" Jim said in exasperation. His surroundings were quite different from the last two. First the classroom, then the playground, but now. . . inside a clock tower? There were gears everywhere, all kinds of gears, all working together to make the clock precisely accurate.

Suddenly, a shadowy figure leaped out from behind one of the gears. "Howdy there, partner! You ready for some gear education?"

"Sure, I'm guessing the gear ghost, right?" replied Jim.

"Right you are," said the ghost. The ghost quickly launched him to the top of the tower and proceeded to explain all about gears: driver gears, follower gears, even rack and pinion gears.

At the end of his lesson with the gear ghost, a vortex appeared and sucked him in without warning. After a couple of seconds, he was quickly sent to his room, and returned to the position he was in before on the bed. In front of him were the three ghosts. The Ghost of Pulleys stepped forward, took a deep breath and said, "Use the knowledge you have just learned to assist you in daily life."

Then the Ghost of Levers stepped forward and said, "Do not forget what we have taught you."

And finally the Ghost of Gears stepped forward and said, "I reckon we could do this again sometime. We'll be here if you're ever in need." The three ghosts quickly huddled together and before you could say, "Mechanical advantage," they disappeared.

Jim sighed and then climbed into his bed. "Wow," he said, "I really need to lay off the junk food."

Figure 6.1 Craig's narrative about mechanical advantage and simple machines

Activity 2: Using plot to communicate content knowledge

Students who want to create their own plots, rather than do a twist on a familiar story, might find the mystery genre useful for communicating content-area information. The content concepts can be used to solve the mystery or can be part of the mystery. The following example was written by Nashanthi, an eighth-grade girl from the same class as Craig (figure 6.2). She used drawings and description to communicate information about levers and pulleys. The mystery provides a context for using these simple machines.

A class discussion of Nishanthi's story might begin with questions such as the following:

- Where do you see evidence that Nishanthi has included information from her science class in her story? What contributions do the science concepts make to the plot?

- What do you learn about the concepts?

- What questions are unanswered? What could Nishanthi have done to give readers a better understanding of what the science terms mean?

- What did Nishanthi do to make the story entertaining? What else could she have done?

- How might you use a mystery to write about the concepts you have just learned? Would the mystery be solved using the concepts or would the concepts be part of the mystery? If a mystery would not work, what other type of story might work better?

Following the discussion, students could look at the notes they have taken of the content concepts they are to incorporate in a narrative. They would consider how they might use the mystery genre to suit their content-area purposes, or they could choose another genre that would be more suitable.

The Case of the Missing Baby

Detective Starling sat in her office. She was about to leave when suddenly a lady walked into her office. "My baby is gone! Please find her for me. She's my only child!" Starling could see that this lady was really upset. "Don't worry, lady. I'll find your baby for you," she said. The lady gave Starling her address and then walked out of her office.

Starling went to the lady's house. She knocked on the door and asked where the baby was when it had been kidnapped. The lady showed Starling to the basement. She looked around and then she found an open window. Under the window she found a metal box and some gears. She opened the back of the box and put the gears on some nails that were inside the box. As Starling began turning one of the gears, the other gears began turning, too. A huge bang came out of the box and then a note flew out of the box. On the note was written:

If you ever want to see your baby come to the old factory at midnight and bring two hundred thousand dollars with you. Don't try anything funny or else...

This note was written by: Dr. Lever

Starling had no other choice but to go to the factory.

Starling walked into the dark factory. She came earlier than midnight so that she could set some traps.

She looked around and found an old piece of wood and some bricks. She put eight bricks at the bottom and then put the piece of wood on top of them. Starling then went to look for something heavy to put on top of the inclined plane. The only thing she could find was an old TV. She pushed it up the piece of wood. It was easier to do than she had thought.

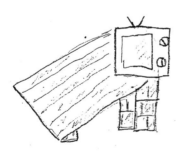

Next, Starling found an old flagpole. She took one end of the rope on the flagpole's pulley and tied it around a nearby box. She took the other end of the rope and made a circle with it.

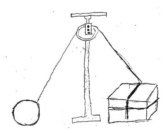

Midnight came and Starling thought that no one would come. Then, she heard some footsteps. They were getting closer and closer. She decided that it was time to use her first trap. When she thought that Dr. Lever was close enough, she pushed the TV off the inclined plane. She heard someone go, "OUCH!!!" She hoped that the baby had not been hurt.

She then ran to the flagpole and held on to the end she had tied to the box. She waited until the kidnapper's foot was in the right place. She pulled on the end of the pulley. The other end went up and she could feel some weight on it. She had caught the kidnapper! The baby had escaped from Dr. Lever when he was hit by the TV. The police came and arrested Dr. Lever and the baby was returned to her mother.

And so, the case was solved thanks to Starling's quick thinking and her grade eight science teacher who taught her everything she knows about levers, gears and pulleys!

Figure 6.2 Nishanthi's story weaving in science concepts

Activity 3: Using character and setting to communicate content knowledge

This activity is a variation of the previous activities, as it shows students how one student has integrated social studies information about the lifestyles of two classes of people in Ancient Greece through characters' interactions and through descriptions of where they live. Students might respond to these questions after reading Jessica's story (see figure 6.3):

- Where do you see evidence that Jessica has included information from her social studies class in her story?

- What do you learn about the lifestyles of the wealthy class, the free labourers, and the slaves?

- Describe the characters and the setting. How did Jessica teach readers about lifestyles of people in Ancient Greece through her story?

- What questions are unanswered? What could Jessica have done to give readers a better understanding of the lifestyles of the three groups of people who lived in Ancient Greece?

- What kind of information can be communicated through describing characters and setting?

- What did Jessica do to make her story entertaining? What else do you think she could have done?

Jessica's Story
Life in Ancient Greece

"Pericles, your father is waiting for you," his mother warned. Don't make him late for the Assembly."

Pericles ran to the door. Clutching his leather hoop and clay ball. He closed the door of their sun-dried brick house and stepped into the street. This was the first time he was going to his cousin's new house. His father said Pericles could play with his cousin all day while his father was at the assembly where citizens debated and passed laws.

Pericles trotted beside his father he noticed all the women with slaves as their chaperones. Soon they where in the market. Suddenly, he saw a man whipping the slave who sold fish in his stall. He stopped to watch what was happening. Not noticing that his father had kept walking.

"That's the last time you'll run away from me, Pandora. I don't know why I bring you to market. From now on, I'll keep you locked up in the house doing housework," the man cried as he whipped Pandora hard along her back.

Pericles looked around to tell his father that they should do something to help. But he only saw peasant farmers selling food from the land they had inherited or got as a reward for serving in the military.

"Great," thought Pericles, now how am I supposed to get to my cousins house?"

He saw Pandora looking defiantly at her owner. She threw a fish on the table peasant woman to buy. Her owner turned around to serve the woman and Pandora ran as fast as she could into the crowd. Pericles watched her dart behind a cart piled high with olives.

"Where did she go?" her owner roared.

"She went in that direction, sir," Pericles pointed in the opposite direction. The man lumbered of. He left the unfree labourer. Who worked to pay off a debt he owed the man to sell the fish.

Suddenly, Pericles' father was standing over him. "So you've been standing here all along, Pericles. Why didn't you follow me? I was almost out of the market before I realized you weren't beside me."

"Sorry father," Pericles said. "I was watching some people. I should have stayed closer to you."

Pandora watched everything that happened. She nodded to Pericles as he and his father walked past the cart she was hiding behind. Then she walked off to a new life. She was no longer a slave because her owner never found her again.

Figure 6.3 Jessica's narrative weaves in social studies knowledge

Following the discussion, students can look at their notes about the content concepts they intend to demonstrate in a narrative. They should determine whether it would be possible to communicate the information through the setting and the characters.

Mini-Lessons: Developing Characters, Plot, and Style

Donald Graves (1994, p.304) observed that in many students' stories, the "characters exist for the plot." Students often write their characters into plots that mirror events in their lives or those drawn from television, movies, or video games. They frequently use a pronoun to refer to the character or may introduce ubiquitous characters, such as the "tall blonde haired girl," who showed up in countless grade six stories on standardized tests.

Yet, as Ralph Fletcher (1993, p.56) writes, "character remains preeminent. The characters contain the crucial human link, that element of human destiny, for the reader to identify with." To become better fiction writers, our students must go beyond referring to a character as "he," "she," or "I." They must go beyond using a stereotypical physical description again and again. The first two activities in this chapter are designed to help support students develop their characters. In one activity, a planning framework helps students think about personality traits for their characters. In the second activity, students analyze how published authors use dialogue. Students can start developing a list of ways they can write dialogue that develops character and moves plot forward.

With other activities, students become aware of possibilities for beginning and ending their stories through analyzing published stories on topics that fit within content-area curricula. Teachers and students also revise some sample bare-bones descriptions to determine how writers might use details to create a sense for readers that they are entering the scene. The final activity uses film to help students recognize the differences between showing and telling what is happening.

Activity 1: Allowing characters to lead the way

In the past, I asked students to begin planning their stories by thinking about the plot. Planning pages were filled with rectangles and circles for students to write what the initiating event would be, how the characters would be thwarted at every turn as they tried to resolve the conflict, and what actions would ultimately lead to resolution. These plot-structure charts ended up as plot-structure ruts that students seemed unable to dig themselves out of. The end result was that many students rewrote the plot structure chart as a story. Their stories were just a string of events.

Clearly this approach lacked the flexibility for students to be creative. In rethinking my approach to supporting students in writing narratives, I drew on the recommendations of published authors. Many say that they start writing their narratives by getting to know their characters. Certain characters will only do certain things, so knowing the characters is important in developing the whole story.

To help students get to know their characters, I suggest giving students the option of using a framework when thinking about potential characters for their narratives (see figure 6.4). Students do not have to use the framework if they already have ideas for their characters – it is a tool for those who need support. Students may answer the questions to create their characters. In addition, they do not have to answer every question in the chart. Some questions might be more appropriate for the characters the students create.

Each question about the character has the potential for determining how the plot will develop. For example, questions about what stands out about the characters and about the characters' problems/motivations/goals will likely be helpful in determining the initiating events for the plot. The characters' personalities, their strengths and weaknesses, or unique physical features, may provide ideas for how the characters will interact with each other to create or help resolve the conflict.

Developing Characters

What are their names?					
What roles do they play in the story? (e.g., protagonist, sister/brother/ friend of protagonist, villain)					
How do they stand out from others?					
What are their goals/problems/ motivations?					
Do they have physical features/ gestures/ facial expressions that are unique? What are they?					
What personalities do they have? Do they have strengths? Weaknesses? What are they?					

Figure 6.4 Template for developing characters

Activity 2: Developing characters and plot through dialogue

Dialogue is one of the hardest parts of writing a story. My students and I try to write dialogue that is as natural as possible. We try to weave it into the narration seamlessly, to make sure that what characters say is consistent with their actions and intentions. It is a tall order. We run the risk of slowing down the story's progress too much if we use dialogue too often, or if a conversation goes on for too long.

Published authors wrestle with the same problems as they write their stories. Our students can learn a lot about writing dialogue when they spend time analyzing published writing. This analysis helps students develop a repertoire of techniques for their own dialogue writing.

In this activity, students work with a partner or in a small group to read the dialogue from books that they are already reading, or from the annotated list in figure 6.5. They might act out the roles of characters to bring the dialogue to life. Students then identify:

1. the kind of information the dialogue provides

2. what kinds of words and expressions make the dialogue seem natural

3. what is written before and after the dialogue so that it seems to fit well with the rest of the passage

4. how long the dialogue is (e.g., how many lines)

5. how many characters are involved in the conversation

6. how the author structures the dialogue (e.g., what words the author uses for "said," how often the author attaches the speaker's name to the dialogue, and how the dialogue is indented)

To develop an extensive list of ways to use dialogue to develop plot and character, students can put their notes together with those of the rest of the class. They can then take a look at their own narrative writing and think about where dialogue would be useful in developing characters or plot. They can think about how much information the dialogue should provide, who will be involved, for how long it should go on, and so on. Figure 6.6 can be used to record students' analyses of the dialogue they read, or it can be used as an overhead transparency if you wish to do this activity as a whole class.

Ho, M. *The Clay Marble*. New York, NY: Farrar, Straus and Giroux, 1993.

The dialogue on pages 3 and 4 introduces the characters and the context of life in Cambodia in 1980.

In this story, a 12-year old girl and her family flee their war-torn Cambodian village and make their way to a refugee camp on the Thai-Cambodian border.

Lawrence, M. *The Gladiators from Capua*. London, UK: Orion Children's Books, 2004.

Students might find it interesting that the dialogue is enclosed in single quotation marks, because the book was published in the United Kingdom. The short, snappy dialogue on pages 29-30 moves the story along and establishes the characters' roles.

This mystery story is set in Rome at the time of Emperor Titus.

L'Engle, M. *A Wind in the Door*. New York, NY: Farrar, Straus and Giroux, 1973.

On pages 3-5, characters and their idiosyncrasies are introduced through dialogue. The adventures in this science-fiction story take readers into outer space and the world of a mitochondrion.

Sachs, M. *The Bears' House*. New York, NY: Puffin, 1971.

On pages 63 and 64, Miss Thompson, Fran Ellen's teacher, asks questions about things that seem out of place in the household, and Fran Ellen does her best to answer truthfully without arousing her teacher's suspicion.

This book is about relationships, imagined and real, in the life of a fourth-grade girl who, because of the failings of the adults in her home life, takes on care-giving roles that demand far more than a 10-year old should have to assume.

Yee, P. *Dead Man's Gold and Other Stories*. Toronto, ON: Groundwood, 2002.

The dialogue on pages 13-14 establishes the context for the story. There are some instances of characters thinking aloud, as well.

The ghost stories are written in the style of traditional Chinese folktales. They tell of Chinese immigrants making new lives for themselves in North America.

Yep, L. *The Traitor: Golden Mountain Chronicles*. New York, NY: HarperCollins, 2003.

Action and dialogue are skillfully woven together on pages 206-207.

This story, narrated by fictional characters, tells of the true-life 1885 massacre of Chinese miners who were hired to replace striking miners in Rock Springs, Wyoming.

Figure 6.5 Annotated list of books providing models for dialogue

How Authors Use Dialogue in Narratives

Instructions: Read the dialogue aloud with a friend, taking on the roles of the characters. Then complete the chart for each conversation you read.

Title of story	Kind of information the dialogue provides	Words and expressions that seem natural	What is written before and after the dialogue	Number of lines of dialogue	Number of characters involved	How often the speaker's name is attached to the dialogue	"Said" words

Figure 6.6 Record of how authors write dialogue

Activity 3: The challenge of details

Details, details, details! Every standardized scoring guide for writing seems to have some mention of the use of detail and description. Details are important to give readers a sense of what the writer is trying to say. Many students seem to be intent on giving the bare bones of the plot so that they and their readers do not get bogged down in details. These students are often the struggling writers and are also often the boys in the class. They argue that too much detail makes a story boring. It certainly is possible to have too many details that end up distracting readers from the main story. Sometimes the most conscientious students (who are often good writers) include so many details that I find myself lost in the description.

Too little detail, though, makes the reader work too hard to figure out what is really happening and who the characters really are. Too much detail forces the reader to work too hard digging through the detail to get at the essence of the story. Sometimes an over-detailed story is almost insulting to readers, never mind boring. As readers, we like to work out some things for ourselves. The over-detailed story is like a movie with characters who tell each other what they are going to do before they do the action. They voice their opinions of each other, for example, leaving nothing for the viewer to figure out. When writing, the trick is to include enough detail so readers can follow what is going on, and yet, to also leave some gaps so that readers can use their background knowledge and experience to create their own images and impressions. Roland Barthes (1975) calls this "writerly text."

Helping students recognize writerly text might involve presenting an example of a bare-bones version of a paragraph from published fiction. Use the example in figure 6.7a, or create a threadbare version of a story that you use in your subject area. Ask students to work with you or, work in small groups to revise the sentence in figure 6.7a by adding details to show readers what it was like for Chu, the character in Paul Yee's short story, *Spirits of the Railway*. Then read the paragraph that Paul Yee wrote (figure 6.7b). Discuss what it means to add details that help readers picture what a situation is like for characters.

- What images do you have of winter from the single sentence? From Paul Yee's paragraph? From your paragraph?

- What details did Paul Yee use to help you imagine what the winter was like for Chu? What details did you use?

Instructions:

Add details to the following:

Winter was hard for Chu. _____

_____

_____

_____

_____

_____

Figure 6.7a Details to add to a sentence

Paul Yee's Details

Then winter came and halted all work. Snows buried everything under a heavy blanket of white. The white boss went to town to live in a warm hotel, but Chu and the workers stayed in camp. The men tied potato sacks around their feet and huddled by the fire, while ice storms howled like wolves through the mountains. Chu thought winter would never end.

(*Spirit of the Railway*, p.13)

Figure 6.7b Paul Yee's details

The same could be done with an overdressed paragraph from published fiction. Use the example in figure 6.8a or create an "overstuffed" version of your choice of fiction. This time, ask students what information is helpful in creating images and what they might cut because the excessive detail is getting in the way of the story.

Instructions:

Revise: Cut unnecessary information.

The crew put up their tents very quickly so they could get to work. They tried to find a level spot to lay out the black ground sheets. They needed hammers to pound in the tent pegs. Many of the pegs were bent, and the tents had a lot of holes. The men worried that their blankets would get wet in the rain. They didn't like the white bosses telling them what to do all the time. Chu thought the white bosses were mean. He felt like talking back to them, but knew he would get into trouble if he did. The men worked very hard and didn't talk to each other.

Then, all of the tents were up, and it was time to go to work. They had to make a pathway for the trains that would be steaming through some day. The men knew they might never be rich enough to ride the trains, but they hoped their children would be able to ride them some day. Chu and the other men climbed a hill and started working away at scooping out the dirt to make a path. They used picks to loosen the rocks and tree roots. Then they scooped the rocks and roots up with shovels. They threw the rocks and roots down the side of the mountain, grunting with the effort. It was hard work, and they didn't get paid very much for it. But at least things weren't all that expensive like they are today, so they could still save some money to send to their families in China. They had sore arms after a few hours, but they kept working.

Figure 6.8a Excessive details that need to be cut

Paul Yee's Details

The crew pitched their tents and began to work. They hacked at hills with hand-scoops and shovels to level a pathway for the train. Their hammers and chisels chipped boulders into gravel and fill. Their dynamite and drills thrust tunnels deep into the mountain. At night, the crew would sit around the camp-fire chewing tobacco, playing cards and talking.

(*Spirits of the Railway,* p.12)

Figure 6.8b Paul Yee's version

After students revise the extremely detailed paragraph in figure 6.8a, ask:

- From the long version, what images do you have of the work that Chu and the crew did? From Paul Yee's paragraph (figure 6.8b)? From your paragraph?

- What details did Paul Yee use in figure 6.8b to help you imagine the work that Chu and the crew did?

Writing Narrative Across the Curriculum • 103

- What details did you keep and which did you cut in the overstuffed paragraph? Why did you keep those details and not others?

Students can then read what they wrote to a peer, and get feedback on where more detail is needed and the places where too many details get in the way of the message.

Activity 4: Beginnings (leads) and endings

One of the challenges of writing narratives is determining how the stories should begin. Writers have many choices. Of the many possibilities for leads, writers might describe a character's ordinary life and what happens to change her/his life. They might create a mood or foreshadow an event. Another consideration for writing story leads is where to start the story in the chronology of events. Stories do not have to begin at the beginning. Sometimes more suspense is created when a writer starts at the end or somewhere in the middle and uses flashback to bring readers forward in time.

A second challenge is how to resolve the problem and how much further the story line should move after the problem is resolved. In order to help students write resolutions to the problems they created for their characters, ask:

- Should the protagonist deal with the problem himself/herself or enlist the help of others?

- Should all the readers' questions about how the protagonist fares be answered? Should a few questions be left unanswered so that readers can decide what happens for themselves?

- What should happen to the antagonists? Should they be shown forgiveness or mercilessly punished (or something in between)?

- Should the protagonist resume ordinary patterns of life that were in place before the story began, or should she/he move on to another setting as a changed person?

Published authors have responded to these questions without digging their characters into such deep holes that mass destruction is the only way to end the story. (Have you noticed that many of our students resort to such endings?) These authors can provide our students with a repertoire of ways to answer the questions about ending narratives.

In this activity, students analyze how authors of picture books begin and end their stories. I suggest using picture books because they can be read more quickly for the purpose of the mini-lesson. Also, our students will be writing short stories, not novels, for their assignments. I find that students get bogged down in complicated twists and turns of the plot when they model their plots after those in novels or movies. These students tire of writing the stories before they can move the story line toward a believable conclusion. Picture books provide students with examples of how they might move characters through an event in just a few pages.

Students read a picture book with a partner. There is a short list of picture books that can be used for this activity in figure 6.9. These books both convey information and tell a story. You may also want to find books in your own collection. Students should respond to the questions in figure 6.10 to analyze the lead and the ending of each story. Students then compare their analysis with their peers. They can then draw on their growing repertoire of possibilities for leads and endings when writing their own narratives.

Picture Books that Weave Content into Narratives

Burleigh, R. *Seurat and La Grande Jatte: Connecting the Dots.* New York, NY: H.N. Abrams, 2004.

This biography of Georges Seurat's life highlights one of his best known paintings, *A Sunday on La Grande Jatte* and introduces readers to pointillism.

Kaplan, W. *One More Border: The True Story of One Family's Escape From War-torn Europe.* Toronto, ON: Groundwood, 1998.

In the spring of 1939, the Jewish Kaplan family flees Lithuania, ending up in Canada.

Laurie, P. *Lost Treasure of the Inca.* Honesdale, PA: Boyds Mills Press,1999.

The author tells the tale of his search for lost Inca gold, ransom for an Inca king, on a trek through mountainous Ecuador. Woven through the story is information about the Inca.

Marin, R. *Oscar: The Life and Music of Oscar Peterson.* Toronto, ON: Groundwood, 2004.

This biography of Canadian jazz musician Oscar Peterson introduces jazz concepts, such as improvisation.

Scieszka, J. *Math Curse.* New York: Viking, 1995.

A school-aged girl is cursed when her math teacher informs the class that "you can think of almost everything as a math problem."

Webb, S. *Looking for Seabirds: Journal from an Alaskan Voyage.* Boston, MA: Houghton Mifflin, 2004.

The author chronicles her month-long expedition to the Aleutian Islands in Alaska as she counts seabirds, whose population density can help gauge the ocean's health.

Figure 6.9 Picture books that weave content into narratives

Beginning and Ending Narratives: Questions to Consider

Title of Book: _____

Beginning (Lead)

- What did the author do (e.g., introduce characters, introduce setting)?

Ending

- Did the main character solve the problem himself/herself or get help from others?

- What questions did the ending answer? What questions (if any) did the ending leave unanswered?

- Did the main character go back to ordinary life, or did she/he move on to another setting?

- Did the main character change in any way? How did she/he change?

Figure 6.10 Questions to consider when writing beginnings and endings

Activity 5: Showing and not telling: Using films

When we explain to students the concept of *showing* rather than *telling* readers what a scene, person, or thing is like, we often use words like, "give specific examples to help readers create visual images," or "bring readers onto the scene so they can see what is happening." Apart from showing readers examples of published authors (Peterson 2003), an effective way to give students a sense of what is meant by "showing and not telling" is through analyzing video clips. Every time we watch a movie, we are being shown what the characters are like. Their actions, responses to one another and the dialogue all give clues to the character's nature.

My favourite video that shows this is called *The Sandlot*. It appeals to students of all ages because of its lovable characters and humorous story line (though the gender stereotyping is an issue that you might need to take up with your students). Information about baseball and baseball heroes is woven into the story in an artful way. One character stumbles into awkward situations because of his lack of knowledge of the game. Other characters fill in the gaps in his knowledge, sometimes helpfully and other times more disdainfully.

I recommend showing about a ten-minute clip of the video (this way you avoid copyright infringement) where the personality of a character is demonstrated through his/her actions and conversations with others. After watching the video, ask students:

- How would you describe the character?

- What did the character do or say to give you this impression?

- What did others do or say to the character?

Students can then write a script for the video clip, including information about the characters' actions and what they say to each other. They could also read their own writing with a partner to determine where they are showing readers what a character, scene, or event is like and where revisions are needed to strengthen their writing.

REFERENCES

Barton, B., and David Booth. *Stories in the Classroom: Storytelling, Reading Aloud and Roleplaying with Children.* Toronto. ON: Pembroke, 1990.

Barthes, R., and Richard Miller, Trans. *S/Z.* London, UK: Cape, 1975.

Booth, David, and B. Barton. *Story Works: How Teachers Can Use Shared Stories in the New Curriculum.* Toronto, ON: Pembroke, 2002.

Graves, D. *A Fresh Look at Writing.* Portsmouth, NH: Heinemann, 1994.

Wells, G. *The Meaning Makers: Children Learning Language and Using Language to Learn.* Portsmouth, NH: Heinemann, 1986.

CHAPTER 7

TEACHING WRITING CONVENTIONS ACROSS THE CURRICULUM

> Punctuation adds texture to language. It's like feeling a fine handmade cloth with our eyes closed; we feel the nap, the bumps, the weave. It's good not to worry too much about punctuation in the beginning. But after a while the punctuation becomes part of what we're trying to say.
>
> **(Georgia Heard 1995, p.125)**

YES, WE ALL TEACH WRITING CONVENTIONS

"I don't have to worry about spelling, punctuation, and grammar. This isn't language arts class." How often have we heard students make this proclamation? They seem to associate writing conventions with a subject area, rather than with generally effective written communication. I have found that many students view writing conventions as a tightly-woven net that is cast over their writing, trapping them in rules and expectations. In their minds, the language arts teacher is the only teacher who has license to cast that net.

It is clear that these students are not looking at writing conventions through the same lens as Georgia Heard! She sees punctuation as an interwoven part of any written communication. Punctuation is not a trap for writers, but rather a tool that adds to and becomes part of the fabric of a piece of writing. Because of their widespread use, writing conventions serve as sign posts for readers. They provide familiar ground for understanding what the writing says (Graves 1994, p.191). One challenge for teachers in all subject areas is to show students how their use of conventions helps readers to understand the writing.

As identified in chapter 1, writing conventions vary with the genre and the context. Conventions expected and accepted by peer audiences in text messaging and e-mailing differ from those of formal essays written for a social studies class, for example. E-mailers use abbreviations and punctuation that would not be acceptable, and perhaps not even understood, by a teacher audience. Similarly, the weave of conventions used in poetry writing is generally much looser than that of essays. Yet, there are exceptions. A sonnet, for example, has a tight weave of syllabic expectations that students might find more difficult to manipulate than the conventions of essays. Helping students understand how communication expectations and needs vary with the context is a second challenge for teachers.

In this chapter, I present suggestions for teaching writing conventions with the belief that the responsibility for teaching and assessing writing conventions falls on the shoulders of teachers of all subject areas, not just the language arts teacher. It is important to remember, though, that being responsible for teaching writing conventions does not mean you will have a systematic program that covers all possible grammar, punctuation, and spelling rules. Instead, you will focus instruction on the conventions that appear again and again in students' writing and that students show they are struggling with.

If you teach language arts/English in addition to content-area subjects, you can teach mini-lessons on writing conventions and proofreading to the whole class or make them part of small-group writers workshops. You can also conduct on-the-spot mini-lessons with students. This can be done in conjunction with consultation during writers workshop or during content classes. If you teach only content-area classes, you might teach one or two mini-lessons to the whole class or to small groups during the weeks that are devoted to writing. On-the-spot mini-lessons that respond to individual students' needs are also helpful during these times. In addition, it is worthwhile communicating with your colleagues who teach language arts, to let them know of pervasive convention errors in student writing. It works well to find a way to collaborate in addressing these trouble areas. Language arts teachers may also be interested in addressing the problems by conducting mini-lessons in their own writers workshops.

TEACHING WRITING CONVENTIONS

Two questions arise when I read students' writing that I find hard to understand because of convention errors: What does the writing show about the writer's understanding of spelling, punctuation, and grammar? How can I help the writer expand and refine her/his repertoire of writing conventions? I also think about how I can help the writer recognize the relationship between writing conventions and readers' understanding, and how I can guide students in developing proofreading and editing skills.

This chapter is divided into two sections, accordingly. The first section, directed toward expanding and refining students' repertoires, makes suggestions for teaching writing conventions. The second section provides techniques for developing students' proofreading and editing skills.

Mini-Lessons: Direct Teaching of Writing Conventions

Reading and writing are the foundations for effective use of writing conventions. Whether or not they recognize it, readers have first-hand experience with the ease of understanding that comes from writers' conventional use of spelling, punctuation, and grammar. Their reading creates visual memories of conventional spellings, sentence structures, and punctuation that they can recreate in their own writing. Jan Turbill (2000) tells a story about her nephew shows that the importance of encouraging students' attention to writing conventions when they read. Her nephew spelled technical terms correctly but often misspelled everyday words when he wrote papers for his university courses. He explained that when he read technical texts, he consciously learned spellings of words that he planned to use in his own writing. He looked carefully at the technical words to work out their meanings. He knew that his computer's spell checking program would not catch those words, so it was up to him to check the spellings of the technical words. He did not pay attention to those words that were more commonly used and caught by a spelling program.

Like Jan Turbill's nephew, when our students have been attentive to writing conventions in their reading, they use what they have noticed to make hypotheses about spelling, grammar, and punctuation. Writing provides space for testing out the hypotheses to see how they help or hinder readers' understanding. Having many opportunities to write across the curriculum allows students to apply their hypotheses about writing conventions to a wide range of genres and contexts.

Our teaching of writing conventions does not stop at creating space for lots of attentive reading and abundant time for writing, however. Some students need explicit instruction to help them recognize the conventions as they read, then they need guided practice to apply their learning as they write.

I generally use two types of lessons when teaching writing conventions and proofreading skills. *Inductive teaching* involves investigations of the use of the convention in published writing, analyses of the similarities in the ways that writers have used the convention, followed by making generalizations about using the convention. *Deductive teaching* starts with an explanation of a convention rule and is followed by a search for examples that confirm the rule. Each type of lesson culminates with students applying the rules in their own writing.

The following two *inductive lessons* focus on helping students with common convention errors. To help teach proofreading and editing skills, there are two examples of *deductive lessons.* These techniques can be applied to teaching any convention or writing skill that students find difficult. Following the mini-lesson, either with the whole class, in small groups, or with individual students, the best way to reinforce the learning is to ask students to find uses of the convention in their own writing. They consider where they have used the convention to clarify readers' understanding and where their use of the convention obscures the meaning. Further reinforcement might take place when you assess the student's writing or provide feedback. In these instances, you would highlight where the student's use of the convention helped and where it hindered understanding.

Activity 1: Inductive teaching to differentiate words that sound/look similar, but have different meanings: focus on *it's* and *its*

Students of all ages confuse words that look or sound very similar but have different meanings. Henriksson (2001, p.13), for example, found the following error in a college student's paper:

> *Alexander the Great conquered Persia, Egypt, and Japan.*
> *Sadly, he died with no hairs.*

Such errors, while humorous to readers who have a good sense of what the writer really wanted to say, can be embarrassing for writers. Becoming aware of the meanings and functions of words, and experience with writing and reading the words help to clarify their uses.

The most commonly confused words are:

there/their/they're	to/too/two
your/you're	except/accept
then/than	effect/affect
its/it's	

You could carry out an inductive lesson focusing on any of these word pairs/trios. Figure 7.1 shows the use of the contraction, *it's,* and the possessive form of it, *its.* Students look for examples of each word in the poem, determining what words *its* and *it's* replace in each phrase. They could do the same with any piece of writing appropriate to what you're teaching, as well. They might also sort the examples into two piles, one where *it's* is used and the other where *its* is used. Students then write a generalization to help them remember the differences between the two words and then apply what they have learned by proofreading and editing their writing.

What *it's* or *its* Replaces

Directions: Read the poem about states of matter, noting where *its* and *it's* appear. Write what other words you could use instead of *its* and *it's* in each line.

Three States of Matter

It's all about
temperature and pressure.

Increase temperature or
pressure
on a solid.
Its molecules move faster –
It's becoming a liquid.

Or,
on a liquid.
Its molecules move faster –
It's becoming a gas.

Ice is a solid.
Its molecules stay put.
Ice holds *its* shape.

Water is a liquid.
Its molecules move a little
and take the shape of *its* container.

Water vapour is a gas.
Its molecules bounce around
to fill all available space.

Add or take away
energy.
It's what you do to change
states of matter.

I am a solid,
But I exhale air.
And there's liquid blood in my veins.

Follow up: What is the difference in meaning between *its* and *it's*? How will you remember the difference?

Figure 7.1 Difference in meaning between *it's* and *its*

Activity 2: Inductive teaching of commas

Rules for using commas are not hard and fast. I find that some editors steadfastly apply certain rules with no exceptions, while other editors bend some rules and apply others more vigorously. In any case, the rules were created to make it easier for readers to understand the writing. Clear communication is the basic rule for using commas.

In this activity, students investigate how published writers use commas. They look at the patterns of comma usage to determine principles for using commas in their own writing. You can repeat this activity for different types of writing so students come to recognize the roles that commas play in fiction, informational text, and poetry. To start the activity, make copies of figure 7.2, and distribute them to each student or small group of students. After students compare their notes with the rest of the class, you can draw up a class set of rules for using commas. Use figure 7.3 together as a large group, and assess where the writer's use of commas helped or confused communication. Then, have students proofread their own writing, editing according to the rules.

Investigating Authors' Uses of Commas

Find examples of commas being used in books and magazines. Then look at all the examples in each category, and come up with a rule that explains how the authors have used commas and why you think they used them in this way.

Category 1: Lists of actions or things
Examples: _____
What seems to be the rule for using commas? _____
Category 2: Dialogue
Examples: _____
What seems to be the rule for using commas? _____
Category 3: When there are dates and years
Examples: _____
What seems to be the rule for using commas? _____
Category 4: When there are names of towns, cities, provinces, countries, and states
Examples: _____
What seems to be the rule for using commas?

_____

Category 5: Separating clauses (e.g., There are two clauses in this sentence; one is underlined and the other is italicized: <u>After the students looked for commas in books and magazines</u>, *they figured out the rules for using commas.*)
Examples: _____
What seems to be the rule for using commas? _____
Your Category: In what other ways do authors use commas? Write three or more examples that do not fit any of the other categories, and figure out a rule to explain what the commas are used for.
Examples: _____
What seems to be the rule for using commas? _____

Figure 7.2 Finding rules for using commas

Directions: Read the following dialogue, and identify where the writer has used commas correctly. Think about the rules that the writer has correctly followed in his use of commas.

Circle the unnecessary commas that get in the way of understanding the sentence. Write a comma in the places where you feel commas are needed to make the meaning clearer.

Celine sat up, stretched and slowly got ready for school. She had cereal, orange juice a grapefruit and toast for breakfast.

"You're going to miss the bus" , her mom warned.

"No, the bus driver always waits for me."

"Pass the milk please." That was Raymond, Celine's brother, talking.

He reached across the table because everyone was ignoring him.

"If the two of you would get out of bed when I called you, then you wouldn't have to rush through your breakfast," Celine's mom said.

"You move so slowly that you will probably get to school by November 30, 2020", said Raymond to his sister.

"At least I don't have my shirt on inside out like you do," Celine retorted.

"That's enough, you two. I'm going to ship you off to your grandmother's in Tokyo Japan if I don't see you rushing out that door. Maybe she'll be able to get you moving in the morning."

Celine and Raymond streaked past her to the bus as it pulled up in the lane way.

Figure 7.3 Finding rules for using commas in dialogue

Mini-Lessons: Developing Proofreading Skills

How do the punctuation, spelling, and grammar of a piece of writing influence readers' understanding? We want students to ask themselves this important question as they proofread their writing. Often, this requires that we model techniques and ways of thinking that students can use when proofreading and editing their writing. The following two deductive lessons provide examples of techniques that many students find helpful.

Activity 1: Deductive teaching of proofreading skills for spelling

In Jan Turbill's (2000) research, 200 teachers read an article containing misspelled words and identified a number of strategies that they used when proofreading. Demonstrate these strategies on the piece of your own writing, a piece from one of your students, or the piece in figure 7.4. Copy the piece onto an overhead transparency so the whole class can see and circle the misspelled words. Voice your thoughts about how you know a word is misspelled to show students how you are thinking.

Here are some strategies you might identify as you circle the misspelled words:

- the word looks wrong

- the word does not follow particular spelling rules you know

Here are strategies you might identify for correcting the spelling:

- read on to see if the word was used somewhere else

- reread the word to see if the meaning is correct for the spelling

- use a dictionary

- sound out syllables

  (adapted from Turbill, 2000, p.212)

The "How to Be a Good Friend"
Quiz

Their are lots of things you can do to be a good friend. I no what I'm talking about. I have more friends than enyone I know.

Here is a quiz to teach you how to be the best freind you can be. Choose the best ansewr you can find. The write answers are at the bottom of this page. Good luck! I hope you have fun makeing new friends!

1. When you're lab partner in scince class thinks you should build a tower with Popsicle sticks and you think it should be built with toothpicks, what should you do?

   A. Tell that person to jump in a lake.

   B. Be open-minded and discuss the situation. You might have to compromise and use some Popsicle sticks and some toothpicks.

2. When someone on your soccer team is being told bye other kids that he or she is ugly, what should you do?

   A. Stick up for the person buy telling the other kids to leave her or him alone.

   B. Join in and tell the person that she or he is uglier than a wharthog.

Correct:

1. B

2. A

Enlarge on the photocopier at 121%.

Figure 7.4 Proofreading skills for spelling

Activity 2: Deductive teaching: Using editing symbols

In this activity, introduce simple editing symbols to help students become independent proofreaders and editors. The first step is to introduce students to editing symbols that editors often use (see figure 7.5). Demonstrate how students would use the symbols by editing the piece in figure 7.6, or a piece of your choice, on the overhead projector. After the demonstration, invite students to use the symbols to proofread unedited writing samples. They may use their own writing or figure 7.7.

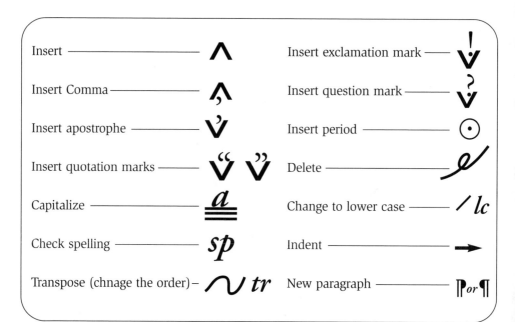

Figure 7.5 Editing symbols

Dear Editor

I think people are driving to much and using up to much gasoline. Gasoline is a non-renewable resources. Non-renewable resources produce carbon dioxide. Which is changing the climate. Have you ever breathed in car exhaust. It stinks right? Thats pollution. Another problem is that gasoline will run out some day. I like being able to drive with my parents to basketball games, like everyone else. But the gas that our car burns cant be used agian. If we use all the gas in the world there won't be gas for future generations to drive they're kids to basketball games We should start car pooling and riding our bikes. If we live in a city, we should take a bus or the subway. All of these things will conserve gas for the future.

Yours truly,

A. Singh
Grade five student

Enlarge on the photocopier at 200%.

Figure 7.6 Demonstrate the use of editing symbols on the overhead projector

The Life of Ray Charles, Father of Soul Music

Ray Charles Robinson was born Sept. 23 1930, in Georgia. He had a terrible thing happen to him when he was just five years old he saw his brother drown in a large laundry tub. You have all seen pictures of Ray charles as an adult and know he was blind. Did you know that he was blind bye the time he was seven years old

Ray learned to read write and arrange music in Braille, and play piano organ, saxophone, clarinet and trumpet at a shcool for the deaf and blind. He started touring the south with dance bands that played in black dance halls. He dropped his last name to avoide confusion with the boxer, Sugar ray robinson. He developed his own style of music. It was like gospel music. With hoots and hollers and non-religious words. He made a hit record in 1954 called "I Got a Woman." This was the begining of a new type of music called Soul.

In February 1958, he recorded a song that sold over a million records called "What'd I Say." In 1961 "Hit the Road Jack" won one of his 12 Grammy awards. Ray Charles also made country music records that were very populer. In 1964 he was arrested. After customs officers found drugs in his coat. Ray Charles took a year off from touring to kick his drug addiction. In 1966 he was given a five-year suspended sentence for drug possession. Ray Charles died on June 10 2004, at the age of 73.

Figure 7.7 For students to practice the use of editing symbols

REFERENCES

Graves, D. *A Fresh Perspective on Writing.* Portsmouth, NH: Heinemann, 1994.

Heard, G. *Writing Toward Home.* Portsmouth, NH: Heinemann, 1995.

Henriksson, A. *Non Campus Mentis: World History According to College Students.* New York, NY: Workman Publishing, 2001.

Turbill, J. "Developing a Spelling Conscience." *Language Arts,* 77(3), 209-217, 2000.

CHAPTER 8

PROVIDING FEEDBACK IN CONFERENCES AND ASSESSING STUDENTS' WRITING

> It's a wonderful feeling when readers hear what I thought I was
> trying to say, but there is no law that they must. Frankly, it is even more
> thrilling for a reader to find something in my writing that I hadn't
> until that moment known was there. But this happens because of who the
> reader is, not simply because of who I am or what I have done.
>
> **(Katherine Paterson 1995, p.34)**

COMMENTS AND GRADES

Like Katherine Paterson, our student writers enjoy getting feedback from readers. They learn about the power of writing by finding out what readers learned, what they got caught up in, and what they found humorous. Students discover more about the intricacies of composing by listening to suggestions for revising or editing particular aspects of their writing. Through writing and receiving feedback, students gain a sense of how well they have understood a concept in a particular content area.

As teachers, we spend a lot of time writing comments to students when assessing their writing. We devote sizable amounts of time to meeting with students, either informally or in pre-arranged student-teacher conferences, to talk about their writing. We hope that our feedback helps students become better at using writing to learn, instruct, entertain, build relationships, direct others' behaviour, or discover more about themselves and their world. We also hope our comments help students gain confidence as writers. We want students to be able to use writing and other communication tools to participate in their classes and in other environments, as well.

One other method of providing feedback, controversial but increasingly unavoidable, is through grades. For many of us, grades are required to report on students' progress. Besides, we find that our students often want a quantitative assessment of the quality of their writing. As a result, we spend time deliberating about whether to assign an "A" or a "B" to a piece of writing. Yet, we know that these grades are not likely to have a huge impact on students' development as writers. Although they give students a sense of how their writing compares to a particular standard, grades reduce our impressions and analyses of the writing to a simple letter or number. The grade on its own does not inform students that their writing is engaging or thought-provoking. The grade does not provide information about how readily we were able to pick up on the writer's main idea. Nor can it even hint at how we enjoyed the words and expressions or how the writing gave us a sense of the writer's voice.

Because grades are increasingly a non-negotiable form of feedback on students' writing, we are constantly searching for methods to grade students' writing and, at the same time, provide more helpful feedback. In this chapter, you will find suggestions for scheduling and carrying out student-teacher conferences, and for assessing students' narrative, non-narrative, and poetry writing in content areas. This is followed by a discussion of research-based recommendations for providing written comments on student writing and for helping students make the most of peer feedback.

TIME ISSUES

Time for Conferencing

Before students submit their writing for grades, they should receive some feedback from you. This could take the form of a few comments provided on the spot while they write. It could take the form of a conversation with students in scheduled student-teacher conferences. It could also come in written form, as you write your impressions on works in progress that students hand in to you before the due dates. To become better writers and to gain a deeper understanding of the content-area concepts, students need an indication of how well their writing fulfils the intended purpose and to what degree they are understanding the concepts from the subject area.

Scheduling the time for feedback is often a problem. Some students finish a piece of writing in the first week and will be looking for guidance in revising their writing. Others plan and gather ideas and information for the first few weeks and get started on their writing in the third or fourth week. They need help getting started and envisioning a direction for their writing.

If you are a generalist teacher and have 25 or more students in your class, you probably will not be able to have more than one scheduled student-teacher conference with each student during each unit. Do not despair – it is not necessary to read and respond to every student's writing every week. You will likely schedule 10-minute student-teacher conferences each week. I recommend no more than two during a 30- or 40-minute class. In addition take time while students write independently to schedule on-the-spot feedback. Ideally, your scheduled conferences will take place after students have completed at least half of their writing, so you and the student have something substantive to talk about.

If you teach only content-area courses and do not have time for the scheduled conferences, you can still give on-the-spot feedback. You can also ask students to hand in their writing at certain points during the six-week unit, or when they feel they need some feedback. Your written feedback will be particularly helpful if you can also talk to students for a couple of minutes about your feedback.

Working within Reporting Periods

Three or four times each year, you gather assessment information about students' learning and convert it into a number or letter grade for report/grade cards. If you want to be fair to students and base your grades on as much information as possible, you must have grades from many samples of students' work for each reporting cycle. You will need to set a schedule of due dates to allow students adequate time to plan, write, revise, and edit their writing. Establishing a schedule of due dates will be helpful to all students, but particularly to those who tend to get mired in the ongoing writing and revision of one piece of writing for many months. My experience shows that these students actually welcome the imposition of deadlines.

As a subject-area specialist, you can work with students to set due dates for tone to two pieces of sustained writing throughout a six-week unit. Alternatively, you might use a number of samples of quick-response writing (e.g., short answers to questions) and one sustained piece of writing that students work on throughout the unit.

As a generalist who teaches language arts/literacy and content areas, you might ask students to complete two to three pieces per reporting period for content-area grades. They could select either writing that has come from content areas or personal choice writing for their language arts/English grade.

STUDENT-TEACHER CONFERENCES

The student-teacher conference is an invaluable element of writer's workshop that allows you to gather information about your students as learners and writers. In these short one-on-one settings, students have a chance not only to express what is important to their learning, but also to have instruction focused on their specific needs.

Processes of Student-Teacher Conferences

The conferences are most effective when they take place in a quiet corner of the classroom where you and the student writer can spend uninterrupted time. Try to be sure that the rest of the class understands that during writing time, no other students try to get your attention or interrupt. If students need help, they should ask a writing buddy, or make a note of the question/problem to consult with you later. They can then either continue working to the best of their abilities, or read until you are free.

Students should bring their writing and a pen/pencil to the student-teacher conferences. You should bring the student's records of previous conferences and observations of the student's learning, together with books, magazines, or your own writing to use as examples for a mini-lesson. Sticky notes are also useful in these conferences, because they allow the student to write short notes explaining what you and the student decide the student should do next with her/his writing. The students can stick the notes to the appropriate places in their writing.

You can also use sticky notes to record what you and the student talked about. Use the record-keeping sheet (figure 8.1), or simply put the sticky notes in the file folder that you keep for each student. These notes provide reminders and information for reporting purposes, and they present an ongoing picture of the student's development as a writer and a content-area learner. They are also helpful for planning future mini-lessons.

Referring to notes from previous conferences fosters the students' sense of commitment to decisions they make in student-teacher conferences. In addition, you might consider the following when determining a process for carrying out the student-teacher conferences:

- Get the student talking about his/her writing. What does he/she want readers to think/feel/learn?

- Ask the student to find the best part of his/her writing and tell you about it.

- Ask the student to talk about what he/she has learned through writing this piece.

- Summarize what you feel he/she is trying to say in the writing.

- Find out what the student wants help with in order to achieve the desired purpose.

Katie Wood Ray (2001) ends her student-teacher conferences by asking her students to tell what they understood she was saying. This tends to illicit more detailed responses from students that simply asking the closed-ended question, "Do you understand?" She then tells her students, "This is what I'm going to write down about what we've talked about in our meeting." This allows for a clear understanding of what happened in the conference, and means that both the student and teacher understand each other.

Notes from Student-Teacher Conferences			
Name: Dates			
Notes:			
Name: Dates			
Notes:			
Name: Dates			
Notes:			
Name: Dates			
Notes:			

Figure 8.1 Notes from student-teacher conferences

Content of Student-Teacher Conferences

About students' writing processes

In student-teacher conferences, you ask questions, make observations, and voice your impressions and feelings – in short, you carry on a conversation just as you would about any topic that interests you and the student. In this instance, the topic of interest is the student's writing and content-area learning. You will likely balance your need for information about the student's learning with the student's need for feedback and their desire for new challenges in their writing and content-area learning.

Ask what the student is working on to be a better writer. Ask the student to show you where the writing communicates what she/he has learned about the content-area topics. You also want to encourage students to try something new in their writing that they have not tried before.

Figure 8.2 lists some questions you might ask to find out more about the student's writing process.

Questions About the Student's Writing and Thinking Processes

1. What is the writer's purpose/intention for the writing?

2. What does the writer use to gather information for her/his writing?

3. Why did the writer choose this particular genre?

4. How strong a sense does the writer have of what the genre can do to serve his/her purpose?

5. What does the writer use to organize his/her writing (e.g., webs, lists, table of contents, headings)?

6. What does the writer do to incorporate the content-area information (e.g., think about it before considering genre or topic, toss it in at the end, weave it in throughout)?

7. What strategies does the writer use to revise (e.g., reread, ask herself/ himself questions about what makes sense)?

8. Whom does the writer use as a resource person for revising and editing?

Figure 8.2 Questions about writing processes

About students' writing

Of course, you and the student will also talk about the actual writing during the student-teacher conference. Giving positive feedback is immensely important, as it has a huge impact on students as writers. You should point out the positive things you found in the writing (e.g., things that were interesting, entertaining, thought-provoking, emotion-evoking, and so on). These comments should reflect your genuine responses to the writing. You should also identify the content-area concepts that the student has clearly understood and the elements of writing (e.g., style, organization, conventions) that the student has artfully and successfully used.

When making decisions about which elements of the writing or the content-area concepts you will discuss, consider the following questions:

- What elements of writing or of the content area do the student need help with that will likely not come up in whole-class instruction?

- Is there something in the student's writing that indicates that I need to teach a concept again?

- What does the student feel he/she needs help with?

You will only be able to address one or two elements of the writing or the content-area knowledge in the conference. Following are possible topics for your student-teacher conference discussions.

ASSESSING STUDENTS' CONTENT-AREA WRITING USING CHECKLISTS

If you are a subject-area specialist, your emphasis when assessing students' writing will be on students' demonstration of the content area concepts. You will also be concerned about the effectiveness of their writing in communicating the ideas, but the grade you assign for the paper will reflect the student's conceptual learning, to the greatest degree. If you teach both content areas and writing, your assessment will likely be balanced between content knowledge and demonstrations of writing competence.

In my experience, students must be made aware of the scoring criteria before they begin writing. They need to know what you consider important in each writing assignment, so they can focus their learning and their efforts in those areas. Letting students know how they will be evaluated gives students a sense of their audience. In the same way, whenever I write an article for publication in a journal, I always check beforehand the types of articles that are being published in that journal. This gives me a sense of what editors and readers want to see, and then I can adapt my style and the way I approach the writing.

Where appropriate, I invite students to help me put together checklists for assessing their writing. I learn a lot about what students know about writing through their suggested criteria for the checklists. More important, my students have a shared sense of ownership over the assessment process. Most often, students are highly motivated to meet expectations outlined in the checklists they help create.

What follows are assessment checklists (figures 8.3 - 8.6) specific to each type of writing (poetry, narrative, and non-narrative) and a checklist that can be used for any type of content-area writing. The category "Conventions" runs across all genres. The goal within this category is for students to use conventions to communicate clearly. This might mean breaking convention rules for a particular effect. In addition, one criterion that will run across genres is students' effective integration of content-area information in a manner that is appropriate for the genre and the audience.

Assessing Content-Area Writing: Checklist

Content   **Points out of** _____

1. Provides information about all concepts   _____

2. Provides accurate information about all concepts   _____

3. Creates a context that presents a thoughtful and,
    perhaps, new way of looking at the concept   _____

4. Provides specific supporting details consistently, so the
    writing is easy to understand and creative/engaging   _____

5. Consistently shows connections between the concepts   _____

6. Maintains a clear focus   _____

7. Uses multiple sources of information   _____

Organization

1. Beginning and ending clearly identify what the writer is   _____
    trying to achieve

2. Uses the structure of the genre to communicate effectively _____

Style

1. Uses language appropriate for the audience and genre   _____

2. Uses specific words and expressions, a variety of   _____
    sentence structures/line breaks/graphic design
    in a creative and effective way

3. Readers get a clear sense of the writer's voice   _____

Conventions

1. Consistently and effectively uses correct spelling, grammar, _____
    and punctuation

                                              Total   _____

Figure 8.3 General checklist for assessment

Assessing Content-Area Poetry Writing: Checklist

Content   Points out of _____

1. Provides information about all the concepts   _____

2. Provides accurate information about all the concepts   _____
    so it is easy to see that the writer understands the concepts

3. Creates a context that presents a thoughtful and, perhaps,   _____
    new way of looking at the concept

4. Provides specific supporting details consistently, so the   _____
    writing is easy to understand and creative/engaging

5. Consistently shows connections between the concepts   _____

6. Uses multiple sources of information   _____

7. Says a lot with few words   _____

8. If titles are used, they contribute to the overall meaning   _____

Organization

1. Ideas flow smoothly and are easy to follow   _____

2. Line breaks add to the meaning and make the   _____
    poem easy to follow

Style

1. Creates images through one or more of the senses   _____

2. Plays with rhythms and sounds of language   _____

3. Uses language that gives a sense of the writer   _____

4. Uses repetition to emphasize ideas or add to the   _____
    rhythm of the poem

Conventions

1. Consistently and effectively uses correct spelling, grammar,   _____
    and punctuation

                                                                        Total _____

Figure 8.4 Checklist to assess poetry

Assessing Content-Area Narrative Writing: Checklist

Content   Points out of _____

1. Provides information about all the concepts   _____

2. Provides accurate information about all the concepts,   _____
    so it is clear the writer understands the concepts

3. Creates a context that presents a thoughtful, and,   _____
    perhaps new way of looking at the concept

4. Supporting details to enhance character development,   _____
    setting, and plot. The writing is easy to understand
    and creative/engaging.

5. Consistently shows connections between the concepts   _____

6. Uses multiple sources of information   _____

7. Dialogue is natural, develops character, and moves   _____
    plot forward

8. Content information is woven into the writing in a way   _____
    that does not disrupt the flow of the story

9. Story has a clear focus and is easy to follow   _____

Organization

1. Story events and ideas flow, are clearly connected, and are _____
    easy to follow

2. Lead provides sufficient information to bring readers into   _____
    the story in an engaging way

3. Satisfying ending ties events together   _____

Style

1. Specific words and expressions engage readers   _____

2. Use of language gives readers a sense of the writer   _____

3. Uses a variety of simple, compound, and complex sentences   _____

Conventions

1. Consistently and effectively uses correct spelling, grammar, _____
    and punctuation

                                                          Total _____

Figure 8.5 Checklist to assess narrative writing

Providing Feedback in Conferences and Assessing Students' Writing • 131

Assessing Content-Area Non-Narrative Writing: Checklist

Content   **Points out of** _____

1. Provides information about all the concepts   _____

2. Provides accurate information about all the concepts   _____

3. Creates a context that presents a thoughtful and, perhaps,   _____
    new way of looking at the concept

4. Provides specific supporting details consistently, so the   _____
    writing is easy to understand and creative/engaging

5. Consistently shows connections between the concepts   _____

6. Uses multiple sources of information and includes references   _____

Organization

1. Beginning and ending clearly identify what writer is   _____
    trying to achieve

2. Maintains a clear focus   _____

3. Uses the structure of the genre to communicate effectively   _____

4. Uses headings, table of contents, borders, and graphics to   _____
    communicate clearly

Style

1. Uses language appropriate for the audience and genre   _____

2. Uses specific words and expressions and a variety of   _____
    sentence structures in a lively and effective way

Conventions

1. Consistently and effectively uses correct spelling, grammar,   _____
    and punctuation

                                                            Total _____

Figure 8.6 Checklist to assess non-narrative writing

ROLE OF SELF-ASSESSMENT

Viewing self-assessment as a learning tool, I used to ask the students to assign a grade, and I then averaged their grade with the grade I assigned. It did not work very well, though, because students gave themselves a grade that reflected their personality and their needs to a greater degree than it reflected the effectiveness of their writing. Students who were self-effacing gave themselves lower grades than those who needed a good grade to boost their grade point average or those who were extremely self-confident. My students told me that they felt very uncomfortable assigning grades to their own writing.

Although I still believe in the importance of self-assessment, I no longer put students through that agony. Now I ask students to write comments explaining what they wanted to achieve in their writing and how well they felt they achieved their intentions. These written assessments are invaluable to me when I assess the writing. They give me a strong sense of what the students have learned about both their writing and the content-area concepts. If students provided information about specific qualities of writing they were working on and either still struggle with or were successful in mastering, I feel they demonstrated a lot of learning. If they made unsupported assessments using words from the scoring guides in general ways, I feel they demonstrated either a need to learn more about the qualities of writing, or a need to learn how to attend to the nuances of their writing and writing processes. Such a self-assessment could also be an indicator that I must do more to demonstrate the value of writing and of self-assessment to motivate the student. I take students' self-assessments to heart and incorporate them into my assessment of their work.

ISSUES REGARDING TEACHERS' WRITTEN FEEDBACK

Recommendations for Written Comments

There has been a great deal of research on the topic of writing comments on students' writing. While most of the research has been conducted at the post-secondary level, the recommendations that come from this research ring true for grades 4-8 teachers, as well. These recommendations are in figure 8.7. I caution that they might not all be appropriate for every student. Combine these with your own knowledge of your students and your classroom context. This is equally important when making decisions about how to respond to students' writing.

Recommendations for Teachers' Written Feedback
(adapted from Straub 2000)

1. Use a conversational tone, imagining that the student is beside you and you are talking together about the writing.

2. Focus on the content, organization, and purpose. Attend to style and conventions to a lesser degree.

3. Focus on two or three concerns in a given set of comments. Students have a better chance of learning the concepts or skills if they have to attend to only a few at any one time.

4. Respond to early drafts in a different manner than to later drafts. Emphasize focus, content knowledge, and overall organization on the early drafts. Address wording, sentence structure, and writing conventions in later drafts.

Figure 8.7 Recommendations for teachers' written feedback

Writing Assessment Is Subjective

Much of my research has looked at the ways in which teachers assess and respond to boys' and girls' writing. In one study, I looked at the differences in the written feedback that 108 sixth-grade teachers gave to girls' and boys' writing. I found that teachers tended to write more comments that corrected and criticized the writing when they thought the writer was a boy. In contrast, they wrote more open-ended questions when they thought the writer was a girl (Peterson and Kennedy 2006).

In addition, I asked approximately 200 teachers in grades 3, 6, 8, and 9 to read student writing and identify characteristics of the writing that pointed to the writer being male or female (Peterson 1998). They identified writers as girls when they felt the writing was detailed, well organized, and had strong, specific vocabulary and character development, and good use of writing conventions. They assessed the writing very differently when they felt boys had written it, describing the writing as short, lacking in detail and character development, using general vocabulary, and lacking in attention to writing conventions. The teachers were talking about the same pieces of writing. The only things that differed were their perceptions of whether the writer was female or male!

These perceptions did not translate into grading patterns that favoured girls, except in one instance. In this case, teachers who felt that the writer was a girl scored the writing higher in every scoring category than teachers who felt the writer was a boy. In addition, in one or two cases, the scores that teachers assigned to the writing ranged from a level 1 (below the acceptable standard) to a level 4 (exceeds the acceptable standard). Teachers seemed to have very different ideas of what constituted good writing.

I present these results to remind you that assessing writing is a subjective process. I do not believe we should see this as a weakness, however. Making personal meaning and bringing in background experiences, perspectives, and values are natural to any reading endeavour. What is important is that we reflect on our experiences and values and become aware of how they will influence our assessments of students' writing.

I believe that my research shows the need to use many samples of writing to assess each student's grade. It also shows the importance of talking with other teachers about their perceptions of good writing. You might get together with other teachers at your grade level from time to time, for example, to mark writing from each other's classes. As you compare the grades you assign to each piece of writing, you will get a sense of the range of perspectives you have on good writing. If two of you mark each piece of writing, you might then average the two scores to determine a final score for the writing.

ISSUES REGARDING STUDENTS' FEEDBACK

What Peers Can Offer

Our students gain a strong sense of audience and gain a wide range of ideas and perspectives when they get peer feedback. Some researchers claim that peer feedback is more genuine than teacher feedback, because it is not connected to the final assessment of the writing (Gere and Stevens 1985). Through peer feedback students become aware of what readers are making of their writing.

In my research in an eighth-grade class, I observed that four types of peer feedback strongly influenced students' drafting and revisions of their writing:

1. The writer and her/his peers played with ideas for the writing.

2. Peers asked for clarification.

3. Peers showed emotional response to the writing.

4. Peers questioned the plausibility of particular ideas or events.

As they wrote, students asked questions of peers sitting close to them and tossed out ideas for deliberation. They seemed to use the talk to explore ideas. Although peers' indications of where the writing was unclear led to some revisions, feedback that questioned the plausibility and showed emotional response was particularly powerful in shaping the writing. The students were concerned about appearing foolish or incompetent in terms of their knowledge of the world and of what was acceptable within the classroom social network. Students were saved potential embarrassment by having an opportunity to negotiate the social meanings within a less threatening small-group setting before reading their writing to the whole class in "Authors Chair." In the following section, I present recommendations for providing opportunities for peer feedback, taking into account the impact of classroom social relationships on students' views of themselves as writers and members of the classroom social group, and how that impacts their writing.

Establishing Routines for Peer Feedback: Some Recommendations

Authors Chair and authors groups, structures within writers workshop, provide opportunities for peer feedback. In these settings, some students flourish and others wilt, often depending on their confidence and competence as writers and their social popularity in the classroom.

Authors Chair, for example, provides an ideal audience for students' writing. I have observed many students delighting in their classmates' attention and acclaim for their writing. I also know some students who reluctantly complete a piece of writing or write something safe that they know peers will accept in order to avoid embarrassment during Authors Chair. Some students, such as those in research conducted by Timothy Lensmire in a third-grade class (1994) and by Pam Gilbert (1993), used their writing to hurt other students and assert their social status in the classroom. In these studies, socially powerful students included characters in their narratives that resembled particular classmates. These characters acted in humiliating ways that embarrassed the peers they represented. I am rethinking Authors Chair because of this research and my own observations in classrooms.

Authors Chair does not have to be a class-wide performance of the students' writing. Students could conduct readings of their writing to small groups of trusted classmates, or they could read to small groups of students in younger grades. Students could also record audio or video of their writing, and have the tapes available for peers to listen to or view in the classroom library. Students could read selected parts of their writing, skipping parts that they wish to keep private. In addition, students should not be required to read every piece of writing to the class. A good rule of thumb is that students have choices about their audiences. Participating in a whole-class Authors Chair should not be the only option.

There are other reasons for rethinking the practice of Author Groups. Donald Graves (1994, p.133) observed that, "Children ask questions before they have thought long enough to understand the text, and most of their questions are of the pro forma type: 'What's your favourite part? What will you write next?' It is almost as if the children have adopted formulaic questions irrespective of the actual piece the author is sharing." Not only can some students feel uncomfortable about giving and receiving feedback from peers, the usefulness of the feedback can be limited if students in a particular group are not committed to helping their fellow writers.

In a previous book (Peterson 2003), I recommended bringing together groups of three or four students to read their drafts to each other and take turns describing effective features and what was unclear or confusing. Since that time, I have had more opportunities to observe students giving and receiving feedback. My research has shown that the most valuable peer feedback is given in two settings: (1) spontaneously while students are writing and (2) when a teacher sets aside time for students to exchange their writing with a partner of their choosing. During this time, the teacher gives the students general questions to get them started talking about each other's writing. These questions include: What did you get out of the piece? What stands out about the piece? What questions does the writing raise for you? One teacher, Andrew, demonstrated how writers need genuine feedback on the clarity, plausibility, and engagement of their writing. He established how to work with peers to show respect and applaud writers who try new things. These types of practices helped students get useful feedback from peers while the complexities of social relationships within classrooms remained respectful.

REFERENCES

David, J., and S. Hill. *The No-Nonsense Guide to Teaching Writing.* Portsmouth, NH: Heinemann, 2003.

Gere, A. R., and R. S. Stevens. The language of writing groups: How oral response shapes revision. In S. W. Freedman (Ed.). *The Acquisition of Written Language: Response and Revision,* 85-105. Norwood, NJ: Ablex, 1985.

Gilbert, P. A story that couldn't be read. In P. Gilbert (Ed.), *Gender Stories and the Language Classroom,* 11-36. Victoria, Australia: Deakin University Press, 1993.

Graves, D. *A Fresh Perspective on Writing.* Portsmouth, NH: Heinemann, 1994.

Lensmire, T. *When Children Write: Critical Re-visions of the Writing Workshop.* New York: Teachers College Press, 1994.

Paterson, K. *A Sense of Wonder: On Reading and Writing Books for Children.* New York, NY: Plume, 1995.

Peterson, S. *Guided Writing Instruction: Strategies to Help Students Become Better Writers.* Winnipeg, MB: Portage & Main Press, 2003.

———. Evaluation and teachers' perceptions of gender in sixth-grade student writing. *Research in the Teaching of English, 33(2),* 181-208, 1998.

Peterson, S. and K. Kennedy (submitted). Grade-six teachers' feedback on girls' and boys' narrative and persuasive writing. *Written Communication.*

Straub, R. The student, the text, and the classroom context: A case study of teacher response. *Assessing Writing, 7(1),* 23-55, 2000.

Wood Ray, K. *The Writing Workshop: Working Through the Hard Parts (and They're All Hard Parts).* Urbana, IL: NCTE, 2001.

CHAPTER 9

SUPPORTING STRUGGLING WRITERS

> Writing is no trouble: you just jot down ideas as they occur to you. The jotting is simplicity itself – it is the occurring which is difficult.
>
> **(Stephen Leacock)**

FINDING IDEAS AND BUILDING A KNOWLEDGE BASE FOR WRITERS

Stephen Leacock was rather cavalier about difficulties that writers encounter. Some of the students in our classes might say that it was easy for him to be clever about what makes writing difficult – he wrote countless books and has a humour award named after him. They would not disagree that seeking out ideas is onerous, however. It is just that their list of writing difficulties does not end there. Our struggling writers often worry about producing something of interest to readers. Some students may be learning English as a second language, in addition to learning to write. Others may be afraid to write what is important to them for fear of peer ridicule. Some of our struggling writers labour with the physical act of moving a pen along a page. They toil with the forms and conventions of writing. These students often try to avoid writing and struggle with it throughout their school years.

Finding ways to support our struggling writers involves considering both their cognitive needs and their social needs. Helping students find ideas for their writing and modelling ways to develop characters and punctuate sentences correctly go a long way to nurture our students' writing development. We must also think about the social environment in which our students are writing. This involves showing students how important writing is in their lives and sending constant messages about writing being important to us. It also involves aligning the purposes for writing closely with those beyond the school. Another consideration is the impact of writing on students' social relationships within the classroom, especially when they are sharing their work. To begin this chapter, I suggest ways to support students' writing development. Next, I move into ways to support students as social beings who navigate the complexities of social lives within and beyond our classrooms.

In content-area classes, finding ideas for writing is no longer a problem because the content-area concepts set parameters on the topics. Yet, if students are to generate ideas to write on content-area topics, they still need to draw from a deep well of information and experiences. Reading, interviewing, observing, experimenting, and surveying are the best ways to fill that well.

After students have start writing, they should be encouraged to continue to gather information through reading, interviewing, observing, experimenting, and surveying. Gathering information does not take place only at the beginning of a writing project. The initial planning and note taking rarely provide all the information needed to complete an article, letter, or book on a content-area subject. In my own experience in writing, I find that after awhile it becomes evident that there are gaps in what I know about the topic. I have to seek out further information to answer new questions that have come up while writing. Student writers in your content-area classes will likely find similar needs as they write. When they are stuck for ideas, they may find it helpful to seek out information on the Internet, in books or magazines, or through interviewing someone in the school or someone who lives and works outside the school.

Struggling writers may need support in identifying and organizing the information they need (see chapter 3 for suggested mini-lessons). The information comes from the many hands-on experiences that you plan for the whole class and the books, articles, and web sites that the students read throughout a unit. When we teach writing in content-area classes, we can pick up on students' unsuccessful attempts to make sense of a topic in the first drafts of their writing, rather than at the end of a unit when students hand in an exam. Students' writing is a mirror of their understanding (or misunderstanding) of a topic. This is clearly demonstrated in the following sentence, written by a college student: "Actually, the fall of empires has been a good thing, because it gives more people a chance to exploit their own people without outside interference" (Henriksson 2001, p.130). Likely to generate a few chuckles, this sentence also signals the student's struggles to understand the concepts. Through ongoing monitoring of student writing, we can catch these kinds of misunderstandings early on and help clarify concepts. Conferencing with students provides both the opportunity to clarify inaccurate understandings of concepts and support for students' writing development.

DIFFICULTIES WITH CONVENTIONS OF WRITING

For the most part, students' struggles with spelling, punctuation, grammar, and the forms of various genres arise from a simple misunderstanding of the conventions. Often, explicit instruction is needed to help students recognize and become comfortable with the spelling, punctuation, and grammar conventions. Practice in using the conventions takes place most naturally when students have ample opportunities to write and edit their own and others' writing.

Chapter 7 provides a range of suggestions for teaching and reinforcing the correct use of writing conventions. Following the mini-lessons, students who struggle with writing may need reminders to help them apply the conventions in their writing. References might take the form of posters or personal notebooks that have examples of the punctuation, spelling, and grammar generalizations that students learn in mini-lessons.

In addition, writing on computers seems to highlight the need for punctuation. Alice, a grade 5/6 social studies teacher, observed that when her students edited their writing on computers, they added punctuation, such as quotation marks, more consistently than when they wrote with pen and paper. She felt that the computer screen made it easier for students to see the need for punctuation marks.

My research on writing assessment shows that many teachers tend to correct every convention error they see in students' writing. This not only results in a huge amount of time being spent on marking students' writing, it creates such a burden on the struggling writer. Regardless of the colour of the ink, a blanket of corrections laid on a piece of writing overwhelms and often paralyzes struggling writers. Where do they start when it seems that everything has to be redone? I have found that it is best to focus on one or two types of errors and to praise students for the writing conventions they have used correctly. If students direct their attention to correcting one or two types of problems, there is a much greater likelihood that they will learn the spelling, grammar, or punctuation rules and use them in future writing.

PHYSICAL AND MENTAL EFFORTS REQUIRED

Grasping and manipulating a pen or pencil requires some students' full concentration. They have little energy left for communicating ideas. Computers have made the physical task of writing easier for these students, freeing them to think about the messages they want to communicate, rather than to how they will form the words. In addition, revision, a labourious exercise when students work with a pen or pencil, is much quicker and less distracting on a computer.

Often, students struggle with writing because it requires so much focused attention. These students welcome short writing assignments and often prefer answering questions or writing short paragraphs. We do not have to deny these students the experiences of discovery writing, however. Poetry provides a forum for students to play with and develop ideas in a short form. The teaching suggestions in chapter 5 encourage a view of poetry as meaning-laden and free struggling writers to communicate something important to them about the content-area topic.

Graves (1994) and I have found the opposite to be true, as well. Some students have no trouble sustaining their focus on writing. Instead, they have trouble completing their writing. I observed a grade-six girl, Shelbi, who wrote a neverending horse story. Fifty single-spaced type-written pages were the result of continuous work on the story from September through May. One day I dropped the photocopy I had made of her story and the unnumbered pages scattered all over the floor. I could not put that story back together again. There were many redundancies, and the flow of the story was very hard to follow. Shelbi, herself, told me that she wished she had had some deadlines for her writing. In the previous year, her teacher had required her to complete a number of pieces of writing each term, and she had finished a number of pieces. Working with students to set deadlines for their writing is a reasonable way to place some boundaries on the time they spend on any of their pieces. In content classes, these deadlines often coincide naturally with the end of a unit of study.

LEARNING ENGLISH AS A SECOND LANGUAGE

Students learning English as a second language (English language learners or ELLs) are learning English vocabulary and sentence structures at the same time as they are learning to write. Although ELLs develop *conversational* fluency fairly quickly, they need much more experience and support in developing English *writing* proficiency. Everyday conversation is often made of short, disjointed phrases using a limited number of high-frequency words. Writing places much greater demands on ELLs, because it requires complete sentences, well-organized paragraphs, and specific vocabulary to develop ideas.

In addition, it is important to be aware that some classroom writing assignments may be culturally inappropriate for some students and may make them uncomfortable. Qi and Smith (2003) give the example that in some cultures, children never oppose an older person's opinion because it draws undue attention to the child. Asking such students to compose an opinion piece that counters the opinion of an adult they know places them in a difficult position.

ELLs have learned a great deal about how language works and about the content-area concepts through learning to speak and write in their original language. Research has shown that ELLs might use this knowledge by writing in their mother tongue and then translating it into English (Kobayashi and Rinnert 1992). They can, alternately, think of the words they want in their first language and then translate the words when they write them (Qi 1998). Some struggling ELLs may benefit from having bilingual colleagues, parents, outside tutors, or peers who share their language to help them translate. The ELLs write what they can in English and then use their first language to express the rest of what they want to say. Alternatives to writing, such as drawing and labelling, or giving oral presentations, are helpful when ELLs are first learning English. Students should move into more complex writing as quickly as possible, however, because they need to develop writing skills to communicate their learning across the curriculum (Smith and Qi 2003).

The teaching suggestions throughout this book draw on published literature and show ELLs many ways to express themselves in writing using the English words, sentence structures, paragraph organizations, and spelling in various contexts. ELLs also benefit from writing by using a number of genres. Through writing and getting feedback from peers and teachers, ELLs can practice and refine what they are learning about using English to communicate their ideas.

When assessing ELLs' writing, we need to pay attention to the message and content of the writing, as well as to the spelling and grammar errors that indicate the students are still learning English. When following the suggestions in chapter 8 for conferencing and assessing writing, you will need to balance considerations for furthering students' proficiency in learning English, as well as their competence in writing and their concept learning.

MOTIVATION TO WRITE

Often, we confuse a lack of motivation for writing with a student's struggle to write. A half-page essay from a student, following weeks of class time devoted to writing, may not be evidence of the student's struggle with writing. Instead, this may signal a student's resistance to writing or a lack of motivation to write.

Research on motivation for writing shows that interest, relevance, and a sense of purpose are critical to engaging students in writing (Pajares and Johnson 1994). My own observations provide yet another example. The other day I was in a sixth-grade science class. Fifteen minutes into a class devoted to writing, two boys who had been kicked out of class the previous week for misbehaving were sitting together drawing lines on blank paper. As I had observed in the previous class, they were resisting getting started on their writing. I found out that they both loved basketball and had thought about writing a story that would include motion concepts. This had proven to be too difficult – they could not find ideas for a story. I suggested that they write a manual on how to play basketball. One boy's eyes lit up as he said, "We could write about playing basketball on Mars!" For the rest of the class time, the two boys wrote furiously. Though they had initially planned to write together, by the end of the 40-minute period, one boy had written two paragraphs of a story and the other had written five tips on playing basketball on Mars. Their enthusiasm for the topic pulled them past their initial resistance to writing.

Assigning open-ended writing projects provides space for students to tap into their interests and knowledge base. You might leave the choice of genre open to students or you might free students up to write whatever they want on a topic as long as they demonstrate their knowledge of a particular concept of study. You might also encourage students to bring in the multimedia and digital technologies that they use outside the classroom. Students might create PowerPoint presentations to demonstrate their learning, for example. They might also use digital video clips or digital pictures and create web sites to communicate what they have learned.

A Desire to Write Is Often Socially Motivated

Enthusiasm for writing is generated when students use classroom writing for their own social purposes (Blair and Sanford 2004; Dyson 1993, 2003). Students build relationships with peers and gain status within the peer social network by, among other things, naming their characters after classmates, or by using humour or grotesque details to entertain their peers. The more broadly we define a topic and genre for students, the more space we create for students to achieve the academic goal and, at the same time, commandeer the writing to achieve their own goals.

Tapping into students' desire for social participation might involve providing the option for students to collaborate with peers when they write. I find that writing in pairs is optimal, since larger groups demand sophisticated social and communication skills that are often beyond students' abilities. It might also involve inviting students to write pieces that they can perform, such as choral speeches, plays, readers theatre, and radio or puppet plays. Students enjoy the favourable attention they get from peers who vie for roles in the performances and who are entertained by the performance. On countless occasions, I have observed delight and satisfaction on students' faces as peers show enjoyment of something they have written and performed. This is infinitely more motivating than writing a paper for a letter grade and a few comments from a teacher.

Although I advocate inviting students to weave their social purposes into their classroom writing, I also caution against giving students carte blanche in their writing. Sometimes students' social purposes include hurting and distressing peers. For example, a socially popular third-grade girl in Lensmire's (1994) study embarrassed a boy who had upset her and humiliated a socially unpopular girl in the class by writing a story in which the boy was the love interest of the socially unpopular girl. This girl's lack of social success was underscored in the story by her desire to grow "zits" to attract boys. In such situations, we cannot be blind to the damage caused by students commandeering their classroom writing for their own social purposes. We need to monitor their writing and place restrictions on content that might embarrass or hurt classmates. Discuss the consequences of their writing with students. Read books and participate in drama activities in the class that are designed to develop empathy. These types of activities may help communicate the message that students should be respectful of peers and not use their writing to harm classmates in any way.

Tapping into students' social needs and desires also involves giving boys and girls space to express their masculinity or femininity in their writing. This issue has come to our attention in the past few years because writing test results show that many boys are not developing the writing competencies that most girls are. This disparity might be attributed to boys' resistance to conform to teachers' and test designers' expectations for writing. Often, these expectations favour a more feminine style of writing – lots of description and detail, conformity to writing conventions and organizational structures, and the absence of violence.

In my research (Peterson 2001, 2002), boys and girls in grades four and eight explained that boys ran the risk of being ridiculed by peers if their writing took on feminine qualities. Because of the more widely respected position of boys' topics, themes, and characters, boys felt that they needed to write in ways that clearly identified them as masculine to others in their classroom. Girls felt that they could write about topics and in styles that were considered feminine or masculine and not suffer great ridicule and embarrassment, however. Supporting boys' and girls' social needs might involve opening up the accepted forms of writing to those preferred by boys and many girls. This includes:

- writing that has the quick pace of an action movie or cartoon

- writing that contains exaggerations, slapstick humour, absurdities and sound effects for audience appeal

- writing that shows loyalties to popular youth culture (Newkirk 2002)

These features might also be incorporated into the checklists that we use to assess students' writing. Often, the writing styles and features that boys have developed to demonstrate their masculinity and develop social relationships within the classroom social network are not recognized in our feedback on their writing.

Daly, Salters, and Burns (1998) caution that gender stereotypes may be strengthened when students follow their gender preferences exclusively, however. Some teacher intervention is needed to introduce students to a wide range of possibilities for their writing. In White's study (1990), for example, small groups of girls who wrote science fiction and adventure stories for younger boys used domestic themes and wrote about the characters' emotional responses to the adventurous situations. Small groups of boys who wrote fantasy stories for younger girls cast female characters in humorous and dangerous positions as tomboys. Typically, boys do not include female protagonists in their writing. Teacher intervention can help persuade both boys and girls to venture away from the stereotypes. Teachers might also introduce literature in which adult writers have crossed gender lines. They can invite discussion about gender stereotypes and the restrictions they place on male and female writers.

REFERENCES

Blair, H., and Sanford, K. Morphing literacy: Boys' Reshaping their School-based Literacy Practices. *Language Arts, 81*(6), 452-460, 2004.

Daly, P., J. Salters, and C. Burns. Gender and task interaction: Instant and delayed recall of three story types. *Educational Review, 50(3)*, 269-275, 1998.

Dyson, A. H. *Social Worlds of Children Learning to Write in an Urban Primary School.* New York, NY: Teachers College Press, 1993.

Dyson, A. H. *The Brothers and Sisters Learn to Write: Popular Literacies in Childhood and School Cultures.* New York, NY: Teachers College Press, 2003.

Henriksson, A. *Non Campus Mentis: World History According to College Students.* New York, NY: Workman Publishing, 2001.

Kobayashi, S., and C. Rinnert. Effects of First Language on Second Language Writing: Translation Versus Direct Composition. *Language Learning, 42,* 183-215, 1992.

Newkirk, T. *Misreading Masculinity: Boys, Literacy and Popular Culture.* Portsmouth, NH: Heinemann, 2002.

Pajares, F.K., and M. J. Johnson. Confidence and Competence in Writing: The Role of Self-efficacy, Outcome Expectancy, and Apprehension. *Research in the Teaching of English, 28,* 313-331, 1994.

Peterson, S. Gender identities and self-expression in classroom narrative writing. *Language Arts, 78(5),* 451-457, 2001.

_____. Gender meanings in grade eight students' talk about classroom writing. *Gender and Education, 14*(4), 351-366, 2002.

Qi, D. S. An inquiry into Language-switching in Second Language Composing Processes. *Canadian Modern Language Review, 54,* 413-435, 1998.

Smith, M., D. Qi. A Complex Tangle: Teaching Writing to ELL Students in the Mainstream Classroom. In S. Peterson (Ed.), *Untangling Some Knots in Teaching K-8 Writing,* 52-65. Newark, NJ: International Reading Association, 2003.

White, J. On Literacy and Gender. In R. Carter (Ed.), *Knowledge About Languages and the Curriculum,* 181-196. London, UK: Hodden and Stroughton, 1990.

APPENDIX A

SAMPLE UNIT PLANS AND ASSESSMENT OF STUDENT WRITING IN CONTENT AREAS

INTEGRATING NARRATIVE WRITING IN SOCIAL STUDIES: SAMPLE UNIT PLAN AND ASSESSMENT OF STUDENT WRITING

The subject-area objectives are the starting point for planning. Consider the concepts that students are to learn and then think about the best ways that writing can be used to foster students' learning of these concepts. In the first example (see figure A.1), students learn how values and beliefs affected the lifestyles of various groups of people in Ancient Greece. They explore this topic more fully by reading books and looking at websites, and by taking on roles of citizens in drama activities about Ancient Greece. They also go on a field trip to a local museum. They take notes from all these activities using the Note Taking: Complete Sentence Stems template (see figure 3.5, p.29). They further develop and demonstrate their knowledge by writing a story (see figure A.4). Look at and assess students' writing to determine the writing skills you need to teach (writing dialogue, using commas, and so on). These skills, along with helping students to take notes and plan their stories, are the topics for mini-lessons.

Grade 6 Social Studies Greece
Topic: An Ancient Civilization

Subject Area Knowledge: Students will demonstrate an understanding of how values and beliefs in early civilizations affected people's daily lives.

Writing Objectives: Students will write dialogue that is easy to follow and develops character and advances the plot. They will use commas effectively.

Writing Activity: Students will write a story based in Classical Greece that shows how values and beliefs in early civilizations affected people's daily lives.

Activities for Gathering Information: Reading books, using the Internet, drama activity taking roles of citizens in Ancient Greece, field trip. Use the Note Taking: Completing Sentence Stems template to take notes on elements of daily life of various groups of people in Classical Greece.

Mini-lessons:

1. Note Taking: Completing Sentence Stems (see chapter 3, p.29)

2. Allowing characters to lead the way (see chapter 6, p.95)

3. Developing characters and plot through dialogue (see chapter 6, p.98)

4. Inductive teaching of commas (see chapter 7, p.114)

Figure A.1 Sample unit plan

In the following pages, I show how students worked through this unit by presenting the planning pages and writing of one grade-six student, Jessica. She used the template for developing characters (see chapter 6, p.97) and the Note Taking: Completing Sentence Stems template from chapter 3, p.29 to record information about lifestyles in Ancient Greece. I assess her writing, showing how I used the checklist for assessing narrative writing from chapter 8, p.131.

Jessica's Notes
Note Taking: Completing Sentence Stems

Topic: How class structure affected the way in which people living in Classical Greece were able to meet their needs

Sources Used: www.historyforkids.org/greekciv/dailylife/htm;
Moulton, C. (Ed.). *Ancient Greece and Rome.* Princeton, NJ: Charles Scribner's Sons 1998.

I learned that Greeks owned slaves that were prisoners of war. These slaves did the work in the fields, in the households, in government, in the mines, and in the marketplace. Some slaves had highly developed skills.

I will show readers how some unfree labourers worked to pay off debts.

My readers will need to know that Greek women couldn't vote or own property. Rich women could only go out with a slave as a chaperone.

- that peasants were artisans and craftsmen. Many peasants paid rent to a wealthy landowner, though some owned land as a reward for military service or through inheritance.

Figure A.2 Jessica's notes for sample social studies unit

Jessica's Planning Sheet for Developing Characters

Names:	Pericles	Pandora
Who is this character?	son of citizen	slave woman who works in a fish stall in the market
How does the character stand out?	gets lost when father takes him to the market	is trying to run away from her owner because he beats her
What is the character's personality?	kind hearted when he sees others in trouble	intelligent and courageous

Figure A.3 Jessica's plan for writing by developing characters for sample social studies unit

Jessica's Writing:
Citizen's Son Helps Slave Woman

"Pericles, your father is waiting for you," his mother warned. Don't make him late for the Assembly."

Pericles ran to the door. Clutching his leather hoop and clay ball. He closed the door of their sun-dried brick house and stepped into the street. This was the first time he was going to his cousins new house. His father said Pericles could play with his cousin all day while his father was at the assembly where citizens debated and passed laws.

Pericles troted beside his father he noticed all the women with slaves as their chaperones. Soon they where in the market. Suddenly, he saw a man whiping the slave who sold fish in his stall. He stopped to watch what was happening. Not noticing that his father had kept walking.

"That's the last time you'll run away from me, Pandora. I don't know why I bring you to market. From now on, I'll keep you locked up in the house doing housework," the man cried as he whipped Pandora hard along her back.

Pericles looked around to tell his father that they should do something to help. But he only saw peasant farmers selling food from the land they had inherited or got as a reward for serving in the military.

"Great," thought Pericles, now how am I suppost to get to my cousins house?"

He saw Pandora looking defiently at her owner. She threw a fish on the table peasant woman to buy. Her owner turned around to serve the woman and Pandora ran as fast as she could into the crowd. Pericles watched her dart behind a cart piled high with olives.

"Where did she go?" her owner roared.

"She went in that direction, sir," Pericles pointed in the opposite direction. The man lumbered of. He left the unfree labourer. Who worked to pay off a debt he owed the man to sell the fish.

Suddenly, Pericles' father was standing over him. "So you've been standing here all along, Pericles. Why didn't you follow me? I was almost out of the market before I realized you weren't beside me."

"Sorry father," Pericles said. "I was watching some people. I should have stayed closer to you."

Pandora watched everything that happened. She nodded to Pericles as he and his father walked past the cart she was hiding behind. Then she walked off to a new life. She was no longer a slave because her owner never found her again.

Figure A.4 Jessica's writing from sample social studies unit

Assessing Jessica's Writing:
Assessing Content-Area Narrative Writing

Content	Points out of 4
1. Provides information about all the concepts	3
2. Provides accurate information about the concepts, so it is clear the writer understands the concepts	4
3. Creates a context that presents a thoughtful and, perhaps, new way of looking at the concept	4
4. Supporting details enhance character development, setting, and plot. The writing is easy to understand and creative/engaging	3
5. Consistently shows connections between the concepts	4
6. Uses multiple sources of information	2
7. Dialogue is natural, develops character, and moves the plot forward	4
8. Content information is woven into the writing in a way that does not disrupt the flow of the story	4
9. Story has a clear focus and is easy to follow	4

Organization

1. Story events and ideas flow, are clearly connected, and are easy to follow	4
2. Lead provides sufficient information to bring readers into the story in an engaging way	4
3. Satisfying ending ties events together	3

Style

1. Specific words and expressions engage readers	4
2. Use of language gives readers a sense of the writer	4
3. Uses a variety of simple, compound, and complex sentences	4

Conventions

1. Consistently and effectively uses spelling, grammar and punctuation	3

Total 59/64 = 92%

con't

Content

Jessica has included accurate information about members of the peasantry, the citizens of the wealthy class, unfree labourers, and women. She incorporated her notes directly into her writing. (This could be an area for a mini-lesson, as I would like Jessica to learn to use the information in her notes in her own words to a greater degree.) The information about the four groups of people is woven smoothly into the story and the focus of the story is maintained throughout. Jessica teaches readers about Ancient Greece and tells a story at the same time.

She uses dialogue effectively to move the plot forward and explains what is happening (e.g., first sentence sets the scene, the slave-owner's dialogue shows what happened to Pandora and Pericles' dialogue shows how he helped Pandora escape her owner).

Jessica provides some specific supporting details about why Pericles is accompanying his father through the market. I have a fairly good sense of why Pandora and her owner do what they do, but would like more information about Pericles to understand his motives for his actions.

Organization

The characters' actions and the events are generally connected. The problem is resolved, though it seems that the ending is rather abrupt. More information about Pericles' involvement in Pandora's life would fill in the gaps.

Style

Jessica uses specific words and expressions in a lively way (e.g., "warned," "trotted," "defiantly"). Although the sentences are not always punctuated correctly, she uses many complex sentences (e.g., "His father said Pericles could play with his cousin all day while his father was at the assembly where citizens debated and passed laws.") and an effective variety of simple and compound sentences.

Conventions

Jessica's writing meets grade level expectations because her spelling, grammar, and punctuation are generally correct. Errors arise when she does not double consonants of verbs when adding suffixes, for the word "were" and a word that she has not likely encountered often in her reading: "defiantly."

Her punctuation of dialogue is partially correct in most instances. Reinforcement of the generalizations learned in the mini-lesson is needed. Jessica's complex sentences are sometimes separated into fragments, though she punctuates simple and compound sentences correctly and uses correct grammar. (This could be an idea for a mini-lesson, as Jessica could benefit from instruction on ways to avoid using sentence fragments when writing complex sentences.)

Figure A.5 Assessment of Jessica's writing from sample unit

INTEGRATING POETRY WRITING IN HEALTH: SAMPLE UNIT PLAN AND ASSESSMENT OF STUDENT WRITING

In this sample unit plan, students learn about the harmful substances in tobacco, its addictive qualities, and the harmful effects on general health. Students explore this topic more fully by reading books, pamphlets, magazines, and websites, and listening to a health nurse. They take notes on figure 3.7 template. They further develop and demonstrate their knowledge by writing a poem (see figure A.8). Because students have not done previous poetry writing, the teacher teaches mini-lessons on basic poetry writing skills, such as using repetition and creating titles for poems, in addition to showing how to use the note-taking format.

Grade 4 Health Topic: Harmful Effects of Smoking

Subject Area Knowledge: Students will identify harmful substances in tobacco, show what "addiction" means, and describe the health effects of smoking.

Writing Objectives: Students will use repetition and write a title for their poetry.

Writing Activity: Students will write a poem showing the health effects of smoking.

Activities for Gathering Information: Students will read books, pamphlets, magazines, and use the Internet. They will hear a presentation by the health nurse and use the Notes and Thoughts template to take notes.

Mini-lessons:

1. How to take notes using a Notes and Thoughts template (see chapter 3, p.31)

2. Using repetition in poetry writing (see chapter 5, p.72)

3. Writing titles for poetry (see chapter 5, p.77)

Figure A.6 Sample unit plan for integrating poetry writing in health

In the following pages, I show how students worked through this unit by presenting the planning pages and the writing of one grade-four student, Ashif. He used the Notes and Thoughts Template from chapter 3, to record information about harmful effects of smoking. I assess his writing using the checklist for assessing poetry writing from chapter 8, p.130.

Ashif's Notes from a Website and Presentation from the Health Nurse

Topic: Harmful effects of smoking
Sources: www.cancer.org/docroot/PED/ped_10_1.asp?sitearea = PED
Health nurse presentation

Notes	Thoughts
• Each year, nearly 1 of every 5 deaths in USA related to smoking.	If everyone quit smoking, there would be a lot more people still alive.
• About 87% of lung cancer deaths caused by smoking. Lung cancer is leading cause of cancer death and one of the most difficult to treat	
• Smoking causes heart disease, lung, larynx, oral, esophagus, bladder, and pancreas cancer	Why would anyone want to take something that is poisonous?
• Tobacco products contain nicotine. Nicotine is addictive and poisonous. More than 60 compounds that cause cancer are found in cigarettes--include ammonia, tar, and carbon monoxide.	
• Carbon monoxide is emitted (400 times greater than what is considered safe in industrial settings). Carbon monoxide interferes with ability of blood to transport oxygen to body.	So that's why people who smoke have a hard time running and climbing stairs and stuff.
• In 1988, the US Surgeon General said that being addicted to nicotine is like being addicted to drugs such as heroin and cocaine.	My uncle has been smoking for 35 years. He says he can't quit. He's addicted.

Figure A.7 Ashif's note taking for sample health unit

Ashif's Poem on Harmful Effects of Smoking: Smoke and You'll be Sorry!

Tobacco has nicotine, nicotine,
Don't know it's addictive –
Where have you been?

Smoking is harmful.
You'll get heart disease and cancer.
Yes sir,
The carbon monoxide messes up
Blood carrying oxygen.
Don't make me say it again.

Tobacco has nicotine, nicotine.
And it is addictive –
You know what I mean!

Figure A.8 Ashif's poem for sample health unit

Assessing Ashif's Poem:
Assessing Content-Area Poetry Writing

Content	Points out of 4
1. Provides information about all the concepts	3
2. Provides accurate information about all the concepts, so it is easy to see that the writer understands the concepts	3
3. Creates a context that presents a thoughtful and, perhaps, new way of looking at the concept	3
4. Provides specific supporting details consistently, so the writing is easy to understand and creative/engaging	2
5. Consistently shows connections between the concepts	3
6. Uses multiple sources of information	2
7. Says a lot with few words	3
8. If titles are used, they contribute to the overall meaning	4

Organization

1. Ideas flow smoothly and are easy to follow	4
2. Line breaks add to the meaning and make the poem easy to follow	4

Style

1. Creates images through one or more of the senses	3
2. Plays with rhythms and sounds of language	4
3. Uses language that gives a sense of the writer	4
4. Uses repetition to emphasize ideas or add to the rhythm of the poem	4

Conventions

1. Consistently and effectively uses spelling, grammar, and punctuation	4

Total   50/60 = 83%

con't

Content

Ashif's poem provides specific information about a few harmful effects of smoking (e.g., heart disease, cancer, blood can't carry oxygen as efficiently). He identifies nicotine and carbon monoxide as harmful substances in cigarettes and cigarette smoke. He uses the word "addictive" but does not show what it means. His notes and thoughts show that he had more information to use in his poem and that he knows what addictive means, but Ashif didn't convey this knowledge in his poem. He had many resources available to him, but chose to take notes only from one web site and the health nurse's presentation.

He uses specific vocabulary related to harmful effects of smoking and his poem is focused on one topic. Ashif has taken the extraneous words out – he does say something with a few words, but there's not a lot of substance to his message. His title clearly gives the message that smoking is harmful.

Organization

Ashif uses line breaks to emphasize important words and to help readers read the poem smoothly. The ideas flow smoothly, and it is easy to follow the message he conveys.

Style

The writing is lively and filled with Ashif's voice. He has done an excellent job of using repetition of sounds and words to enhance the rhythm and the flow of the poem. He uses some specific vocabulary to create visual images of the harmful effects of smoking.

Conventions

Ashif uses punctuation artfully to enhance the meaning of his poem. I showed him how to use the m-dash in a student-teacher conference, and he applied what he learned really well. His spelling is correct throughout the poem.

Figure A.9 Assessment of Ashif's writing from sample health unit

INTEGRATING WRITING OF ANY GENRE OF STUDENTS' CHOICE IN SCIENCE: SAMPLE UNIT PLAN AND ASSESSMENT OF STUDENT WRITING

In this sample unit plan, students learn about levers, gears, and pulleys. They explore this topic more fully by reading books and looking at websites, by classifying every day examples of each, and by hands-on activities making simple machines out of a variety of objects. Students take part in a competition making catapults that shoot wrapped chocolates into a tub. Students take notes on a Cornell note-taking framework in figure 3.9, on page 33. Students further develop and demonstrate their knowledge by writing in whatever genre they choose. Because students can choose any genre, the topics of mini lessons are: assessing the validity of information, proofreading their writing for spelling, and using the Cornell note-taking format.

Grade 8 Science Topic: Simple Machines

Subject Area Knowledge: Students will demonstrate an understanding of:

- mechanical advantage

- types of levers, pulleys, and gears

- how each simple machine makes work easier

Writing Objectives: Students will assess the validity of information they gather and proofread their writing for spelling.

Writing Activity: Students will write using a genre of their choice about two types of simple machines.

Activities for Gathering Information: Reading books and using the Internet, making catapults and other simple machines, classifying everyday simple machines. Students will use the Cornell note-taking framework to take notes.

Mini-lessons:

1. Assessing the quality of information (see chapter 3, p.24)

2. Using Cornell note-taking framework (see chapter 3, p.33)

3. Deductive teaching of proofreading skills for spelling (see chapter 7, p.116)

Figure A.10 Sample unit plan for science

In the following pages, I show how students worked through this unit by presenting the planning pages and the writing of one grade-eight student, Brandon. He used figure 3.9, the Cornell note-taking framework from chapter 3, p.33, to record information about levers and pulleys. Because some students in Brandon's class chose to write narrative, others wrote poetry, and others wrote using non-narrative genres, I assess all students' writing using the general checklist for assessing content-area writing (chapter 8, p.129).

Taking Notes Using the Cornell Framework

Topic: How pulleys and levers work

Sources Used: http://www.sirinet.net/ ~ jgjohnso/simple.html

Questions	Notes
How do pulleys work?	• Pulley is a grooved wheel that turns around an axle (Fulcrum), a rope or a chain is used in the grove to lift heavy objects • Pulley changes the direction of the Force — Instead of lifting up, you can pull down using your body weigh against the load (what you are lifting) Examples — On Top of the Flag Pole to Raise and Lower the Flag, To Hoist a Sail, to Open Curtains
How do levers work?	• Lever is a bar that is free to turn about a fixed point called the Fulcrum. has 2 other parts — force (what you are trying to move or lift) — effort arm - The work done on the lever. • First Class Lever has fulcrum between the effort and load (e.g., seesaw, scissors) Effort goes down in order to lift the Load. • Second Class has the load between the effort and the fulcrum. Produce a gain in force. Ex. wheelbarrow, bottle opener • Third Class has effort between load and fulcrum. Loss in force, but gain in speed and distance. Examples: broom, shovel, fishing pole, baseball bat

Short Summary of Notes

Pulleys are ropes around grooved wheels that change direction of force to lift things. Three types of levers have load, effort and fulcrum in different positions to lift or move things or to produce a gain in force or make things go faster and farther.

Figure A.11 Brandon's notes for sample science unit

Brandon's Newspaper Article: Pulleys Used to Rescue Stranded Whales

There was a large commotion last week at the coast near the town of Fake Lake. A large group of whales had been stranded on the shores of the beach. This presented a problem of not enough space for patrons seeking an afternoon of fun in the sun. The bigger problem was that the rescue team had to return the whales to the water before they died.

They tried every idea that came to their mind, including pushing the whale with a tractor and offering the whale $50.00 to just get up and swim back into the water. All failed miserably. Time was running out when Pat Mercury, a concerned passer-by, proposed that they implement a pulley system to lift and carry the whales to safety. Pat explained that a construction crane would do the work because cranes are designed to lift large amounts of weight.

The rescue workers hooked the whales and raised them one-by-one. They positioned the whales above a safe amount of water, lowered them into the water and detached the hoist. The whales were saved! The rescue team was befuddled as to why they did not think of this earlier. If it were not for a knowledgeable stranger's assistance, the whales would surely have perished. With that in mind, the members of the rescue team resigned, sure that staying on duty would hurt more than help.

Figure A.12 Brandon's writing for sample science unit

Assessing Brandon's Newspaper Article:
Assessing Content-Area Writing

Content   **Points out of 4**

1. Provides information about all concepts   ___1___

2. Provides accurate information about all concepts   ___2___

3. Creates a context that presents a thoughtful and,
   perhaps, new way of looking at the concept   ___3___

4. Provides specific supporting details consistently, so the
   writing is easy to understand and creative/engaging   ___1___

5. Consistently shows connections between the concepts   ___2___

6. Maintains a clear focus   ___3___

7. Uses multiple sources of information   ___1___

Organization

1. Beginning and ending clearly identify what writer is
   trying to achieve   ___2___

2. Uses the structure of the genre to communicate effectively   ___3___

3. Readers get a clear sense of the writer's voice   ___4___

Style

1. Uses language appropriate for the audience and genre   ___3___

2. Uses specific words and expressions, a variety of
   sentence structures/line breaks/graphic design
   in a creative and effective way   ___3___

Conventions

1. Consistently and effectively uses spelling, grammar,
   and punctuation   ___4___

Total   32/52 = 62%

con't

Content

Brandon had much more information about levers and pulleys in his notes than he was able to incorporate into his newspaper article. (I will plan mini-lessons teaching students how to incorporate content information into newspaper articles and narratives in the next unit.) He created an interesting context for using a pulley and provided some accurate supporting details about how pulleys work, but did not include any information about levers. The article was focused on the rescue of the whales, and there were connections between ideas. There aren't many science ideas, so I cannot get a good sense of the connections he is making between science concepts. Brandon used only one source of information for his notes.

Organization

Brandon introduces the whale problem in the first paragraph, shows how the rescue workers tried to solve the problem in the second paragraph and then explained how they finally rescued the whales in the final paragraph. The title also summarizes the main idea of the newspaper article. In this respect, Brandon used the structure of the genre quite effectively. He just did not clearly achieve the purpose of demonstrating what two simple machines are and what they can be used for.

Style

Brandon uses specific language, such as "stranded," "patrons", and "construction crane" and readers get a clear sense of his voice through the humorous ending. There is a variety of sentence structures, as Brandon uses compound, complex and simple sentences. He uses short sentences for effect (e.g., "The whales were saved!"). He uses an appositive correctly.

   The tone and language are generally appropriate for a newspaper article, though some details seem more narrative-like, than newspaper article-like (e.g., "This presented a problem of not enough space for patrons seeking an afternoon of fun in the sun.")

Conventions

Brandon uses punctuation, spelling and grammar effectively to make it easy for readers to follow his ideas. Even the less commonly-used words are spelled correctly and the complex sentences are punctuated correctly.

Figure A.13 Assessment of Brandon's writing for sample science unit

BOOKS THAT INCORPORATE CONTENT INFORMATION: GRADES 4-8

Science

Anderson, L. *Beavers Eh to Bea: Tales from a Wildlife Rehabilitator.* Winnipeg, MB: Turnstone Press, 2000.

Cole, J. *The Magic School Bus Lost in the Solar System.* Markham, ON: Scholastic, 1994.

_____. *The Magic School Bus Plays Ball: A Book About Forces.* Markham, ON: Scholastic, 1998.

_____. *The Magic School Bus Explores the Senses.* Markham, ON: Scholastic Canada, 2001.

Drake, J., and A. Love. *The Kids Book of the Far North.* Toronto, ON: Kids Can Press, 2000.

Fisher, L. E. *Gutenberg.* New York, NY: Atheneum, 1993.

_____. *Alexander Graham Bell.* New York, NY: Atheneum, 1999.

Freedman, R. *The Wright Brothers: How They Invented the Airplane.* New York, NY: Holiday House, 1991.

Lauber, P. *Who Eats What? Food Chains and Food Webs.* Toronto, ON: HarperCollins Canada, 1994.

Simon, S. *The Brain.* Toronto, ON: HarperCollins, 1999.

_____. *Weather.* Toronto, ON: HarperCollins, 2000.

Verstraete, L. *Accidental Discoveries: From Laughing Gas to Dynamite.* Markham, ON: Scholastic, 1999.

Wick, W. *A Drop of Water.* New York, NY: Scholastic, 1997.

Zoehfeld, D. W. *What Is the World Made of? All About Solids, Liquids, and Gases.* Toronto, ON: HarperCollins, 1998.

Social Studies

Blumberg, R. *The Remarkable Voyages of Captain Cook.* New York, NY: Atheneum, 1991.

Coleman, P. *Rosie the Riveter: Women Working on the Home Front in World War II.* New York, NY: Random House, 1998.

Drake, J., and A. Love. *The Kids' Book of the Far North.* Toronto, ON: Kids Can Press, 2000.

Granfield, L. *Cowboy: A Kid's Album.* Toronto, ON: Douglas and McIntyre, 1993.

_____. *Pier 21: Gateway of Hope.* Toronto, ON: Tundra, 2000.

_____. *Where Poppies Grow: A World War I Companion.* Markham, ON: Fitzhenry and Whiteside, 2001.

Greenwood, B. *A Pioneer Story: The Daily Life of a Canadian Family in 1840.* Toronto, ON: Kids Can Press, 1994.

_____. *The Last Safe House: A Story of the Underground Railroad.* Toronto, ON: Kids Can Press, 1998.

Kraft, B. H. *Mother Jones: One Woman's Fight for Labor.* Boston, MA: Houghton Mifflin, 1995.

Levine, K. *Hana's Suitcase.* Toronto, ON: Second Story Press, 2003.

Merritt, S. E. *Her Story: Women from Canada's Past. I, II, and III.* St. Catharines, ON: Vanwell Publishing, 1993.

Moore, C. *The BIG Book of Canada: Exploring the Provinces and Territories.* Toronto, ON: Tundra, 2002.

Schlissel, L. *Black Frontiers: A History of African American Heroes in the Old West.* New York, NY: Aladdin, 1999.

Springer, J. *Listen to Us: The World's Working Children.* Toronto, ON: Groundwood, 1997.

Stanley, J. *Children of the Dust Bowl: The True Story of the School at Weedpatch Camp.* San Jose, CA: Crown Books for Young Readers, 1993.

Tanaka, S. *The Buried City of Pompeii: What it Was Like when Vesuvius Exploded.* Markham, ON: Scholastic, 1997.

Yue, C., and D. Yue. *The Wigwam and the Longhouse.* Boston, MA: Houghton Mifflin, 2000.

Music

Ferris, J. *What I Had Was Signing: The Story of Marian Anderson.* Minneapolis, MN: Lerner, 1994.

Hayes, A. *Meet the Orchestra.* New York, NY: Harcourt, 2001.

Kamen, G. *Hidden Music: The Life of Fanny Mendelssohn.* New York, NY: Simon and Schuster, 1996.

Krull, K. *Lives of the Musicians.* Orlando, FL: Harcourt Brace, 1993.

Raschka, C. *Mysterious Thelonious.* Markham, ON: Scholastic Canada, 1997.

Art

Bonafoux, P. *A Weekend with Rembrandt.* New York, NY: Rizzoli, 1992.

Cech, J. *Jacques-Henri Lartigue: Boy with a Camera.* New York, NY: Simon and Schuster Children, 1994.

Greenberg, J., and S. Jordan. *The American Eye: Eleven Artists of the Twentieth Century.* New York, NY: Dell Books for Children, 1995.

Venezia, M. *Francisco Goya.* Markham, ON: Scholastic Canada, 2000.

Winter, J. *Diego.* New York, NY: Knopf, 1991.

Health

Brown, L. K. *What's the Big Secret: Talking About Sex with Girls and Boys.* New York, NY: Little Brown and Company, 2000.

Farrell, J. *Invisible Enemies: Stories of Infectious Disease.* New York, NY: Farrar, Straus and Giroux, 2005.

Giblin, J. C. *When Plague Strikes: The Black Death, Small Pox and AIDS.* New York, NY: HarperCollins, 1995.

Pavanel, J. *The Sex Book: An Alphabet of Smarter Love.* Montreal, PQ: Lobster Press, 2001.

Mathematics

Anno, M. and M. Anno. *Anno's Mysterious Multiplying Jar.* New York, NY: Puffin, 1999.

Geisert, A. *Roman Numerals I to MM.* Boston, MA: Houghton Mifflin, 2001.

Lasky, K. *The Librarian Who Measured the Earth.* Boston, MA: Little and Brown Company, 1994.

Wyatt, V. *The Math Book for Girls and Other Beings Who Count.* Toronto, ON: Kids Can Press, 2000.